Brotherhood and Sisterhood: A Historical Survey of Special Education Law in Macau, 1991-2014

Wen Ru Jia

Brotherhood and Sisterhood: A Historical Survey of Special Education Law in Macau, 1991-2014

Author   Wen Ru Jia
Editor   Yang Chia Ying
Issuer   Lin Qing Zhang
General Manger   Liang Jing Shing
Editor-in-Chief   Chang Yen Jui
Front cover image by   Pusamam Digital Culture CO.,LTD.
ISBN 978-986-478-786-9   First Printing, 2022.12

WAN JUAN LOU BOOKS CO., Ltd.
6F.-3, No. 41, Sec. 2, Roosevelt Rd., Da'an Dist.,Taipei City 106, Taiwan
TEL (02)23216565   FAX (02)23218698   service@wanjuan.com.tw

作　　者　溫如嘉
責任編輯　楊佳穎
實習編輯　許雅宣
特約校稿　林秋芬
發 行 人　林慶彰
總 經 理　梁錦興
總 編 輯　張晏瑞
發　　行　萬卷樓圖書（股）公司
　　　　　臺北市羅斯福路二段41號6樓之3
　　　　　電話 (02)23216565 傳真 (02)23218698
　　　　　電郵 SERVICE@WANJUAN.COM.TW
ISBN　978-986-478-786-9
2022年12月初版
定價：新臺幣360元

本書為臺灣師範大學國文學系2022年度「出版實務產業實習」課程成果。
部分編輯工作，由課程學生參與實作。

Table of Content

Chapter Five: Uncertainty in the Implementation of Special Education in Macau

List of Charts and Forms in the thesis

Chapter Three: The Influencing Elements for the Development of the Related Special Education Law in Macau

3.1　The Population in Macau

3.1　The Total Area of Macau

3.1　The Population Density of Macau

3.2.1　The Number of Special Education Schools/Institutions in Macau

3.2.1　The Number of Special Education Teachers in Macau

3.2.1　The Student Enrolled Number of Special Education in Macau

3.2.1　The Student Graduated Number of Special Education in Macau

3.2.2　The Details of Students with Special Education Needs from Different Types of Schools

3.2.2　The Details of Students with Special Education Needs

Chapter Four: The Problems Relating to Individuals under the Decree Law No.33/96/M (the Macau Decree Law of Special Education System)

4.1　The Classification of Students with Special Education Needs in the Decree Law No.33/96/M and the Law No.9/2006

4.1.1.3　The Categorization of Students with Special Education Needs in the Laws of the United States, Taiwan and Macau

4.4　The Main Service Details of Evaluation and Consultation

4.4　The Duty for Related Services Provider

Chapter Five: The Uncertainty in the Implementation of the Related Special Education Law in Macau

Table of International Instruments

1. The Salamanca Statement and Framework for Action 1994
2. The Civil Code (Macau)
3. The Law No.11/91/M (Macau)
4. The Decree Law No.81/92/M (Macau)
5. The Decree Law No.33/96/M (Macau)
6. The Decree Law No.33/99/M (Macau)
7. The Law No.9/2006 (Macau)
8. Section 504 of the Rehabilitation Act (the United States of America)
9. The Individuals with Disabilities Education Act (the United States of America)
10. The Taiwan Special Education Law (Taiwan)
11. The Taiwan Enforcement Rules of the Special Education Act (Taiwan)

Abbreviation

1. The Macau Education and Youth Affairs Bureau (the DSEJ)
2. The Centre of Psycho-Pedagogical Support and Special Education (the CPPSSE)
3. The Centre of the Statistics and Census Service (the DSEC)

Chapter One
Introduction

1.1 Background of this research topic

Macau went through three distinct periods in its legal history: a period of mixed Chinese-Portuguese jurisdiction (1557-1849), a colonial period (1849-1974) and a post-colonial period (1974-1999).[1] It is now in its fourth period: Chinese administration under special conditions".[2] Macau is a small place with a total land area measured 29.9 km²,[3] and a population of 582,000.[4] Around 11,141 people out of the total population are disabled.[5] As the development goes by, providing them with a proper education becomes a necessary topic. Special education in Macau keeps a stable pace in development. Legislation lobbying plays an indispensable role in the development of special education in Macau and such legislation can play a major role in solving the issue.

On August 29th, 1991, the Macau government promulgated the Law No.11/91/M. The Law No.11/91/M was known as the Law of the Education System of Macau. Article 13 of Chapter Two (Organization of the education

---

[1] http://ccadvog.com/cc/?p=670; accessed on 8th of July, 2014.

[2] http://ccadvog.com/cc/?p=670; accessed on 8th of July, 2014.

[3] See official statistics, the Centre of the Statistics and Census Service (the DSEC) ed., ENVIRONMENTAL STATISTICS 2012, Macao: DSEC (05/2013), p25.

[4] See official statistics of the DSEC http://www.dsec.gov.mo/default.aspx?nored irect=true; accessed on 2nd of March, 2014.

[5] See official statistics of the DSEC ed., ENVIRONMENTAL STATISTICS 2012, Macao: DSEC (04/2012), p21.

system) in the Law No.11/91/M further described the aims, classification, methods and so on of special education in Macau. On July 1st, 1996, the government published the Decree Law No.33/96/M for a better protection of the education right of the students with special education needs. This Decree Law was known as the Macau Decree Law of Special Education System. It was a law in the development of the Law No.11/91/M.[6] On December 20th, 1999, the government of the People's Republic of China resumed its sovereignty over Macau, Macau has changed rapidly. It was a significant transformation period for adjustment and development for Macau. It was a significant transformation period for the adjustment and the development of Macau. After December 20th, 1999, Macau government published a series of laws based on the situation of the society at that time in pursuit of better regulation for future development. One of them was the Law No.9/2006, the Macau Fundamental Law of Non-Tertiary Education System. The Decree Law No.33/96/M (the Macau Decree Law of Special Education System) is still valid at present. However, nearly two decades went by, the defects of the Decree Law No.33/96/M have become more obvious than ever, and it is not efficient enough to fully protect the education right of the students with special education needs; therefore an updated legislation of special education may be needed. We will focus on the defects of the law of special education in Macau in the subsequent chapters.

1.2 Significance of this research topic

1.2.1 The academic significance

There are a few laws concerning special education in Macau. However,

---

6   The Decree Law No.33/96/M (the Macau Decree Law of Special Education System).

the Decree Law No.33/96/M which mainly regulates special education, is not operational enough. Moreover, the present Decree Law No.33/96/M has defects in the education system. This situation tells us that a new and specific law for special education in Macau is urgently needed. This thesis may actually give a forward-looking perspective for the legislation of future special education law in Macau comparing with the special education laws in other areas around the world, and in the end, promoting the study of Macau special education in the legal aspect may be achieved.

1.2.2 The significance in practice

There are a few obstructions in regulating the practical issues of special education in Macau. The rights and obligations of the individuals concerning special education are not well-regulated in the legal system. The legislation of special education falls far behind from the actual implementation of special education in Macau. Although the practice of special education goes well at present, the procedures to implement special education are not regulated in the legal system and the legal loophole of special education is still a problem. These situations will endanger the education right of the students with special education needs. By renewing the special education law, a lot of hidden dangers can be eliminated. The implementation of special education can be more smoothly in the reality if people can give more attention to the legislation of special education. If we systematically analyze the legal issues, it may be helpful for building up a more effective legal framework. This thesis is trying to systematically analyze the legal issues of special education in Macau, and present more constructive suggestions for the implementation of the laws and regulations in Macau special education.

1.3 Questions provoked

The main purpose of this thesis is to give legislative suggestions regarding special education law in Macau after comparing different special education laws in different areas. More specifically, there are six questions to be solved in this thesis:

a. What is the general situation of the enforcement of special education in Macau?

b. What is the legislative status of special education in Macau? How many laws are related with special education in Macau and what are they?

c. What kinds of individuals care about special education? What are their rights and obligations in the Law No.9/2006 (the Macau Fundamental Law of Non-Tertiary Education System) and the Decree Law No.33/96/M?

d. What are the procedures of implementing special education? What regulations should the individuals involved in the implementation of special education follow?

e. Are the existing laws effective enough for practical issues?

f. From a legal aspect on the legislation of special education in Macau, how to regulate the practical operations effectively in the future?

1.4 Methodologies of this research topic

There are several methods used in the thesis.

First of all, it is the statistics and diagrams analysis method based on the data obtained from the Government of Macau Special Administrative Region Statistics and Census Service (DSEC). Understanding the reflection from the data can help us locate the problem of the legislation of special education in Macau. In this case, by analyzing the data, we could obtain the background of special education in Macau in a general way. Moreover, we can suggest what direction should the legislation of special education in Macau take on in the future.

Secondly, a doctrinal method of the research is adopted. The provisions concerning special education will be discussed separately. A systematic discussion on the provisions will be resorted to analyze the detail of each regulation in the legal aspect of special education in Macau.

Thirdly, in order to look for a better regulation for the practical issues in the enforcement of special education, a comparative study will be used in the thesis. Under some particular cultural background, different areas use different ordinances to regulate how special education is implemented. We can find ways to better improve the special education laws in Macau while studying the special education law from other areas. In this thesis, the special education law in Taiwan and the United States of America are used as a contrast objects.

Finally, in order to achieve the purpose of the thesis, which is to present suggestions to implementing the regulatory framework of special education in Macau, all the methodologies are integrated instead of using them separately.

1.5 Chapter layout

Chapter One will be the beginning introduction of this thesis. It will introduce the background, the significances, main questions and methodologies of this thesis.

Chapter Two will present the major events about the development of special education in Macau. It will be shown in a chronological order. The contents of Chapter Two includes: the first special education school established in Macau will be introduced in the beginning of Chapter Two; secondly, the first time that special education was written in the law of the Law No.11/91/M, which was known as the Law of the Education System of Macau in 1991; thirdly, the establishment of the Centre of Psycho-Pedagogical Support and Special Education (the CPSSE) in 1992 will be introduced, the CPSSE was known as the authorized department from the Macau Education and Youth Affairs Bureau (the DSEJ) for the further management of special education in Macau; next content concerning special education will be the event of the legislation of the Decree Law No.33/96/M It was established on July 1st, 1996, and was known as the Macau Decree Law of Special Education System; after it, there will be the introducation of the Decree Law No.33/99/M so called the Decree Law of the effect on approving the system of Prevention, Rehabilitation and Integration of People with Disabilities; and the last thing will be introduced in Chapter Two is the Law No.9/2006 in 2006 after the People's Republic of China resumed its sovereignty over Macau on December 20th, 1999.

Chapter Three will present some statistics concerning special education in Macau. They include the population, the number of special education school, the number of students with special education needs, and the number of teachers teaching special education and so on. The data will show us a clearer picture of the special education in Macau. And the data will tell us how many aspects are influenced by the Law No.9/2006 and the Decree Law No.33/96/M.

Chapter Four will present the individuals concerning special education and special education law. The major parties involved in the implementation of special education are the students with such needs, their parents, the teachers and the related services providers. Parts of the chapter will compare the special education laws in other countries, and locate some good samples in the hope of seeking the solution for a better legislation of special education. This chapter will discuss the defects of the regulation in the legal system. From this chapter, we find that most of the defects in the legal system are caused by of the legal loophole or the inappropriate regulations of the laws.

Chapter Five will present some more defects of special education law during its implementation. Most of the chapter are related to the procedures of the implementation of special education. The Decree Law No.33/96/M and some other laws concerning the special education fail to keep the pace of the development of special education in practice. The main procedures of the implementation for the special education include four steps:

    a. The identification and referral;

    b. The evaluation;

    c. The development of Individualized Education Plan and Educational Activities Program;

    d. The placement.

All of them are crucial for the students with special education needs. In Macau, there are few articles specifying those procedures, and the present special education laws may no longer be a good influence for the practical special education in Macau. Due to the missing regulations of special education in the legal system, it will cause dilemma and increase the difficulty to protect the education right of the students with special education needs. Furthermore, there are a few uncertainties of the implementation of the Law No.9/2006 and the Decree Law No.33/96/M of special education. Analyzing the laws will be helpful for us to find out what kinds of regulations will benefit the students and protect their education right.

Chapter Six will provide the relevant conclusion as the end of the thesis.

Chapter Two
The Important Events of Special Education Law in Macau

Education right is the right granted by the Universal Declaration of Human Right and the laws from all the countries in the world.[1] In 1989, the Convention on the Rights of the Child was adopted by the United Nation General Assembly.[2] "It enters into force in September 1990 and it becomes the most widely- and rapidly-accepted human rights treaty in history."[3] An unprecedented summit of Heads of State and Government at the United Nations in New York City set ten-year goals for children's health, nutrition and education, in the world summit for Children, 1990.[4] In June 1994, the World Conference on Special Needs Education was held in Salamanca, Spain.[5] During this conference, the United Nations Educational, Scientific and Cultural Organization (UNESCO) adopted the Framework for Action on Special Needs Education and the Conference Statement (The Salamanca

---

[1] See official statistics of the UNESCO http://www.unicef.org/about/who/index_ history.html; accessed on 8th of July, 2014.

[2] See official statistics of the UNESCO http://www.unicef.org/about/who/index_ history.html; accessed on 8th of July, 2014.

[3] See official statistics of the UNESCO http://www.unicef.org/about/who/index_ history.html; accessed on 8th of July, 2014.

[4] See official statistics of the UNESCO http://www.unicef.org/about/who/index_ history.html; accessed on 8th of July, 2014.

[5] See official statistics of the UNESCO http://www.unescobkk.org/education/ inclusive-education/what-is-inclusive-education/background/; accessed on 8th of July, 2014.

Statement and Framework for Action).[6] This Conference reaffirmed the right to education of every individual, as enshrined in the 1948 Universal Declaration of Human Rights, and renewed the pledge made by the world community at the 1990 World Conference on Education for All to ensure that right for all regardless of individual differences.[7] The system and programs of which should thus be designed to take into consideration the diverse characteristics and needs of students with disabilities through creating welcoming and inviting environment in general schools under Salamanca Statement.[8] The education right for children with special education needs is officially recognized worldwide through this conference. The education right is for all regardless of individual differences.[9] This is a big step for the development of special education, and it is the first time that the education right for children with special education need is not just a concept in people's mind, it finally has an international legal meaning by written into the Salamanca Statement. Furthermore, on August 31st, 2008, the Convention on the Rights of Persons with Disabilities of United Nation took effect in China (both Hong Kong special administrative region and Macau special administrative region are included). The purpose of the Convention was to promote, protect and ensure the full and equal enjoyment of all human rights and fundamental freedom by all people with disabilities, and to promote

---

6 See official statistics of the UNESCO http://www.unescobkk.org/education/ inclusive-education/what-is-inclusive-education/background/; accessed on 8th of July, 2014.

7 See official statistics of the UNESCO http://www.unescobkk.org/education/ inclusive-education/what-is-inclusive-education/background/; accessed on 8th of July, 2014.

8 Kim Fong Poon-McBrayer & Ping-man Wong "Inclusive education services for children and youth with disabilities: Values, roles and challenges of school leaders", Children and Youth Services Review, 35 (2013), pp1520-1525.

9 The Salamanca Statement and Framework for Action, 1994.

respect for their inherent dignity.[10] People with disabilities include those who have long-term physical, mental, intellectual or sensory impairments, which, in interaction with various barriers, may hinder their equal rights to fully and effectively participate in social activities.[11] Education fairness is one of the representations of social fairness. Furthermore, education fairness is the extension of social fair and it is one of the prerequisites to achieve social fair. To ensure education fairness, we should admit that everyone has the right to receive education. It is another great improvement for protecting the education right for individuals with special education needs.

On the perspective of the development of special education around the world, the law of special education has always been the most influential factor and the key to propel further advancement. The situation of special education in Macau is no exception. Legal power plays an essential role to improve the development of education. "The rich heritage of Macau is a product of 500 years of interaction between East and West. Macau went through three distinct periods in its legal history: a period of mixed Chinese-Portuguese jurisdiction (1557-1849), a colonial period (1849-1974) and a post-colonial period (1974-1999). It is now in its fourth period: Chinese administration under special conditions".[12]

We can find related legal basis for protecting the rights of students with special education needs from the above legal pyramid in Macau. And the related legal basis is the main topic for the author to discuss in this thesis. This thesis will talk about the development of special education, the recent situation of special education and the defects of the existing special education law in Macau, so that we may find a better way to improve the situation of special

---

10 The Convention on the Rights of Persons with Disabilities of United Nation, Article 1.

11 The Convention on the Rights of Persons with Disabilities of United Nation, Article 1.

12 http://ccadvog.com/cc/?p=670; accessed on 8th of July, 2014.

education in Macau from the perspective of legislation.

If those individuals with special education needs received proper education and related services, they could decide to live a normal life, master their lives, and avoid those unfavorable situations in social life. Because the amount of regular students outnumbers that of students with special needs, special education is easily neglected, thus, it has become the least noticed portion in the education system. The development of the special education is a key element for evaluating the educational level of a specific area. The level of legislation and legal implementation in special education can provide us another perspective to see this problem, and this is the reason why we can start from the related development of special education laws in Macau.

The following paragraphs will show us about the historical development concerning special education laws of special education system in Macau in chronological order.

2.1 The very beginning of special education in Macau

In the 1960s, special education in Macau was absent in the education system. In 1967, a Christian school named São Paulo started to accept disabled students.[13] It was the beginning of official special education in Macau. Till 1988, the school was renamed as Xie-Tong Special Education School in 1988.[14] This was the first special education school established in Macau.[15]

---

13 Special education of Hong Kong, Macau and Taiwan (港澳臺的特殊教育), http://wenku.baidu. com/link?url=RlR3baUGtvuJJJlXPGpn_Tcxng1KVgr9zN7rBUgLwQcQRNsgswlMFzunrv83 __rJNVra_Cz4gUKtJ82G9icxK6ipMkTvnm5SshEZqkKvt1C; accessed on 8th of July, 2014.

14 Special education of Hong Kong, Macau and Taiwan (港澳臺的特殊教育), http://wenku.bai du.com/link?url=RlR3baUGtvuJJJlXPGpn_Tcxng1KVgr9zN7rBUgLwQcQRNsgswlMFzunrv 83__rJNVra_Cz4gUKtJ82G9icxK6ipMkTvnm5SshEZqkKvt1C; accessed on 8th of July, 2014.

2.2 The first written law of special education in Macau

In the mid-1980s, the development of special education in Macau grew rapidly.[16] Macau communities outreached special education, and special education classes, schools and training centers were built up in succession.[17] Special education was broadly accepted internationally and the legislation of special education was issued one country after another. Meanwhile, the group of students with special education needs in Macau was large enough to attract the government to pay more attention to. During that time, Macau was still the colony of Portugal; it was the Portugal government who contributed to the special education legislation in Macau during that period.

On August 29th, 1991, the Macau government promulgated the Law No.11/91/M, known as the Law of the Education System of Macau. Paragraph 1 in Article 4 of the Law No.11/91/M clearly defined that special education was part of the education system in Macau.[18] Even more, Article 13 of Chapter Two (Organization of the education system) of the Law No.11/91/M further described the aims, classification, methods and so on of special

---

15 Special education of Hong Kong, Macau and Taiwan (港澳臺的特殊教育), http://wenku.bai du.com/link?url=RlR3baUGtvuJJJlXPGpn_Tcxng1KVgr9zN7rBUgLwQcQRNsgswlMFzunrv 83__rJNVra_Cz4gUKtJ82G9icxK6ipMkTvnm5SshEZqkKvt1C; accessed on 8th of July, 2014.

16 Ruan Bangqiu, "Macau Special Education: Review and Hope", Administration, Vol. 21, issue 79, 2008 No.1, pp81-104.

17 Ruan Bangqiu, "Macau Special Education: Review and Hope", Administration, Vol.21, issue 79, 2008 No.1, pp81-104.

18 The Law No.11/91/M, Paragraph 1 of Article 4: The educational system comprises: a) The pre-school education; b) The preparatory year for primary education; c) Primary education; d) Secondary education; e) Higher education; f) The special education; g) The adult education; h) Technical and professional education.

education in Macau. It provided a much more completed system for people to follow the regulation than before and helped people to have a better understanding of special education. Although the Law No.11/91/M was abolished in 2006 when a new education law was issued, it was still not hard to tell that the Law No.11/91/M was the milestone for the development of special education in Macau. From the very beginning of the Law No.11/91/M was put into force, there was legal ground for the students with special education needs to rely on. That gave a meaningful progress to the development of special education.

2.3 The establishment of the Centre of Psycho-Pedagogical Support and Special Education (the CPSSE)

After the Law No.11/91/M took effect, special education in Macau was developed rapidly and the assistance from the DSEJ was not enough and efficient any more. A specialized agency was very necessary to be built to tackle those problems related with special education. Under this circumstance, in order to better assist the students with special education needs, an institute authorized by government with scientific and professional knowledge of special education and related services was needed.

On December 21st, 1992, the Decree Law No.81/92/M was issued. This decree law was about setting the current organizational structure for the DSEJ. Because of Article 17 of the Decree Law No.81/92/M, the CPSSE was established. The main duties for the CPSSE were written in Article 17 as follows:[19]

---

19 The Decree Law No.81/92/M (The Decree Law of the Current Organizational Structure for the

a) Set the psycho-sociological framework of criteria in order to characterize the educational needs of students; b) Establish procedures for necessary recovery and promote their application in order for the integration of students in the school and social context; c) Supervise, monitor and evaluate the measures that to be implemented in the school health; d) Plan and implement activities for information and educational and vocational guidance; e) Develop reference frameworks of professions and detect vocational and professional skills, guiding students for further study and career opportunities; f) Establish the general framework of the organization of special education; g) Define profiles of peculiarity and arrange follow-up plan, adapting it to the educational needs of the student; h) Promote the existence of a database on care services for children and youth with disabilities; i) Provide technical and pedagogical supports to the students with special educational needs; j) in conjunction with the Educational Resource Center, organizing the documentation on special education, selecting and disseminating the documentation which can bring interest to educators and families of children and youth with special educational needs; l) Participate in licensing activities of establishments of education for students with specific disabilities, and consider applications to amend the conditions of its operation.

The DSEJ set up a team to cohesively develop special education and better serve those students with special education needs. The team included counselors, social workers, physiotherapists, occupational therapists, pediatricians (concurrent post available as well), child and adolescent pscychiatrists

DSEJ), Article 17; the articles are in Chinese version and Portuguese version; the articles in English version are translated by the author.

(concurrent post available as well).[20]

The establishment of the CPSSE provided a more systematic and scientific services to the students with special education needs than ever before 1992.

2.4 The passing of the Decree Law No.33/96/M (the Macau Decree Law of Special Education System)

Even the CPSSE was established in 1992 and made an impressive improvement for development of special education, Macau still stayed in a position as an area without specific law of special education. This remained a legal loophole and this legal loophole derived the students with special education needs of their legal reliability. Furthermore, the disputes between the wishes to receive proper education from the students with special education needs and the rejections to receive students with special education needs from schools became more and more intense. With these disputes, it was not easy for the CPSSE to do the meditations if no legal basis could be founded to settle these disputes. To make progress of this issue was not easy.

Facing this dilemma and trying to tackle this problem, on July 1st, 1996, the government published the Decree Law No.33/96/M (the Macau Decree Law of Special Education System) for the better protection of the education right of the students with special education needs. This decree law, known as the Macau Decree Law of Special Education System was a law to support the Law No.11/91/M in Macau at that time, because the Decree Law No.33/96/M was for the further development of the legal system established by Paragraph 1

---

20 Chen Fenglian, The General Situation of Macau Special Education, (The Macau Education and Youth Affairs Bureau, 1999).

of Article 13 of the Law No.11/91/M.[21] It approved a special education system for students with special educational needs. The Decree Law No.33/96/M did a profound job in further protecting the right of students with special education needs. And this law is still valid at present. However, as nearly two decades went by, the defects of the Decree Law No.33/96/M became clearer than ever, and it was not efficient to fully protect the education right for the students with special education needs; an updated law of special education may be needed. We will focus on the defects of the law in the subsequent chapters.

2.5 The passing of the Decree Law No.33/99/M (the System of Prevention, Rehabilitation and Intergration of People with Disabilities)

On July 19th, 1999, the Decree Law No.33/99/M so called the Decree Law of the Effect on Approving the system of Prevention, Rehabilitation and Integration of People with Disabilities was passed. The purpose of the Decree Law No.33/99/M (The Effect on Approving the System of Prevention, Rehabilitation and Integration of People with Disabilities) is to prevent from disability and help the disabled to recover and to integrate into mainstream society.[22] Some articles of this decree law further add that special education should be applied in all levels of school and reaffirmed that no prejudice is imposed on the education right of the disabled.[23] This law is valid at present.

---

21 The Decree Law No.33/96/M (the Macau Decree Law of Special Education System); the articles are in Chinese version and Portuguese version; the articles in English version are translated by the author.

22 The Decree Law No.33/99/M (the Macau Decree Law of Approving the System of Prevention, Rehabilitation and Integration of People with Disabilities), Article 1.

23 The Decree Law No.33/99/M (the Macau Decree Law of Approving the System of Prevention, Rehabilitation and Integration of People with Disabilities).

It regulates a variety of the aspects in the society for the disabled in Macau.

We can tell some of the articles have a big effect on improving the situation of special education, such as Article 10 of the Decree Law No.33/99/M:[24]

> 1. *Special education is the education mode teaching in all levels of school, including public and private schools, which aims at the integral development for disabilities with special educational needs, as well as their preparation for full integration in active life.*
>
> 2. *Without prejudice to the provisions of the Law on the Education System of Macau, measures for progressive integration of students with disabilities in the education system should be adopted, and ensure that appropriate responses to be given to the students with disabilities in the situation of long-term stay at home or hospital.*

Furthermore, Article 19 of the Decree Law No.33/99/M:[25]

> 3. *The education system should provide comprehensive responses to children and young people, who have special educational needs, favoring their integration into regular schools or in specialized institutions, where the severity of the case requires, in appropriate*

---

24 The Decree Law No.33/99/M (the Decree Law of the effect on Approving the system of Prevention, Rehabilitation and Integration of People with Disabilities), Article 10; the articles are in Chinese version and Portuguese version; the articles in English version are translated by the author.

25 The Decree Law No.33/99/M (the Decree Law of the effect on Approving the system of Prevention, Rehabilitation and Integration of People with Disabilities), Article 19; the articles are in Chinese version and Portuguese version; the articles in English version are translated by the author.

pedagogical, human and technical conditions.

4. In implementing the provisions of the preceding paragraph, it shall be progressively adopted measures to promote equal opportunities of disabled person to access to and success in education, including through measures of positive differentiation.

It protects the rights and interests for those with disabilities and makes sure the implementation can be carried out well through the education system. Meanwhile, the disputes between students with disabilities and schools are reduced, because the Decree Law No.33/99/M regulates that education system to have the obligation to provide proper education to children and young people with disabilities.

2.6 The passing of the Law No.9/2006 (the Macau Fundamental Law of Non-Tertiary Education System)

Since the Government of the People's Republic of China resumed its sovereignty over Macau on December 20th, 1999, Macau has changed rapidly. It was a significant transformation period for adjustment and development for Macau. After December 20th, 1999, local Macau government published a series of laws based on the situation of the society at that time and for better regulation of the future development; one of them was the Law No.9/2006 which was the Macau Fundamental Law of Non-Tertiary Education System.

Article 12 of the Law No.9/2006 (the Macau Fundamental Law of Non-Tertiary Education System) is a specific part for regulating special education. The contents of Article 12 include the aims of special education, the categorization of who can receive special education, the way for special education's implementation, Individualized Education Plan, the government's duty and the last paragraph.[26] Further more, Article 54 of the Law No.9/2006 is an article for the revocation of the Law No.11/91/M. It regulates that if the complementary law of the Law No.11/91/M does not violate the prohibition or order of the Law No.9/2006, the complementary law of the Law No.11/91/M remains valid until the complementary law of the Law No.9/2006 enters into force.[27] That means except Paragraph 2, 3 and 5 of Article 39 remains valid,[28] the Law No.11/91/M was partial replaced by the Law No.9/2006. The Law No.11/91/M used to be the legal basis of the Decree Law No.33/96/M. At the beginning of the Decree Law No.33/96/M, the statement says that the Decree Law No.33/96/M is one of the established legal system of the Law No.11/91/M.[29] In addiction, the Law No.9/2006 says that special education is subject to a specific statute.[30] The Law No.11/91/M was partial renovated[31] and was replaced by the Law No.9/2006. Article 54 of the Law No.9/2006 makes the Decree Law No.33/96/M to remain as one of the complementary laws for special education[32] under the circumstance that no other law of special education is established.

Comparing the Law No.11/91/M and the Law No.9/2006, with no doubt,

---

26 The Law No.9/2006 (the Macau Fundamental Law of Non-Tertiary Education System).

27 The Law No.9/2006 (the Macau Fundamental Law of Non-Tertiary Education System), Paragraph 2 of Article 54.

28 The Law No.9/2006 (the Macau Fundamental Law of Non-Tertiary Education System), Paragraph 1 of Article 54.

29 The Decree Law No.33/96/M (the Macau Decree Law of Special Education System).

30 The Law No.9/2006 (the Macau Fundamental Law of Non-Tertiary Education System), Paragraph 6 of Article 12.

31 The Law No.9/2006 (the Macau Fundamental Law of Non-Tertiary Education System), Paragraph 1 of Article 54.

32 The Law No.9/2006 (the Macau Fundamental Law of Non-Tertiary Education System), Paragraph 2 of Article 54.

some of the contents of special education were changed. Some of the legal issues had progressive outcomes. There were a lot of improvement of the Law No.9/2006 comparing with the Law No.11/91/M.[33] It changed and improved the regulation of the aims of special education, students with born disabilities, the evaluation, the implementation methods of education, the Individualized Education Plan and the duty of government.

The aims of special education in the Law No.9/2006 are no longer just focusing on ensuring the quality of the education and student's integration of the society like the Law No.11/91/M. The aims of special education in the Law No.9/2006 are to ensure the quality of the education opportunity and student's integration of the society.[34] It shows higher attention to the diversity of the student and provides appropriate education to the students with special education needs.

Students with born disabilities are recognized as the students eligible to receive special education and the related services.[35] This concept of students with born disabilities was not mentioned in the Law No.11/91/M. As far as author's concern, due to Paragraph 6 of Article 12 says that the system of special education is subject to a specific law,[36] it can be predicted that, the further categorization of students with special education needs will be stated in

33 The Law No.11/91/M (the Law of Macau Education System), Article 13; the Law No.9/2006 (the Macau Fundamental Law of Non-Tertiary Education System), Article 12.

34 The Law No.9/2006 (the Macau Fundamental Law of Non-Tertiary Education System), Paragraph 1 of Article 12.

35 The Law No.9/2006 (the Macau Fundamental Law of Non-Tertiary Education System), Paragraph 6 of Article 12.

36 The Law No.9/2006 (the Macau Fundamental Law of Non-Tertiary Education System), Paragraph 6 of Article 12: the system of special education is subject to a specific statute; the articles are in Chinese version and Portuguese version; the articles in English version are translated by the author.

a specific law of special education. However, this is just a prediction and Macau is still staying in the situation that no proper categorization of physical and psychological limitations for students to receive special education and related services is written in the law at present.

About the evaluation of students with special education needs, we can see that it is an obligation for the department or the authorized entities to provide relevant public services.[37] This is good for the students, their parents and schools to look for assistance for students' evaluation and the implementation of the related special education law about this process (evaluation) can be monitored in a more systematic way than the Law No.11/91/M.

The implementation methods of special education in the Law No.9/2006 changed a lot comparing with the Law No.11/91/M. Inclusive education as an important implementation method of special education gets attention from the legislators of the Law No.9/2006 and it has become the preferential way to implement special education in Macau. This is a very important change about the way to teach students with special education needs. Besides, this changed article also shows the attitude of the legislator toward special education. The inclusive education better fits the international trend on the implementation of special education, and it will bring more benefits for all the students in the education system.

No regulation of the Individualized Education Plan was mentioned in the Law No.11/91/M, which was neglecting the importance of the Individualized Education Plan in special education. Due to the importance of Individualized Education Plan for every student with special education needs, emphasizing the Individualized Education Plan in the article means the respect of the

---

[37] The Law No.9/2006 (the Macau Fundamental Law of Non-Tertiary Education System), Paragraph 2 of Article 12.

student's characteristics. The legislation should make details about special education plan like the Law No.9/2006 does.

The conditions of the Law No.9/2006 on "what the government should create"[38] are much more systematic[39] than those of the Law No.11/91/M.

All in all, the replacement of the Law No.11/91/M by Law No.9/2006 is more suitable in the recent situation of special education in Macau; it fits in the international trend, approves some important contents of special education and gives a better guide to the future development of special education in Macau.

---

[38] The Law No.9/2006 (the Macau Fundamental Law of Non-Tertiary Education System), Paragraph 5 of Article 12.

[39] The Law No.9/2006 (the Macau Fundamental Law of Non-Tertiary Education System), Paragraph 5 of Article 12.

Chapter Three
The Influencing Elements for the Development of the Related Special Education Law in Macau

Quantity of elements can influence the development of the legislation of special education. The economic, cultural and political factors are three major factors affecting the development of the law. There are some factors with very general meanings. The chapter will talk about the action and reaction between the related special education law and those elements directly influencing the development of the related special education law.

3.1 The environmental element and the population in Macau

Macau is not a very big place with a total land area measured 30.3km² in 2013.[1] It consists of Macau Peninsula and two islands Taipa and Coloana. "Macau has always been China's sacred territory since ancient time",[2] even it was a Portuguese colony lasting for 446 years. The Government of the People's Republic of China resumed its sovereignty over Macau on December 20th, 1999. The long-lasting colonial times made Macau a society with diverse cultures. Macau is a typical multicultural society combing Chinese traditions

---

1   See official statistics of the DSEC ed., ENVIRONMENTAL STATISTICS 2012, Macau: DSEC (05/2013), p25.

2   Lau Sin Peng, A History of Education in Macau, translated by Sylvia S.L IEONG & Victoria L.C LEI, (Faculty of Education , University of Macau, 2009), p1.

and Western customs. The population in Macau grew from 339,500 in 1990 to 607,500 in 2013.[3] Macau has a not very big population, however, 607,500 people living in a space of 30.3 km² makes Macau a relatively crowded area.

3.1 The Population in Macau[4]

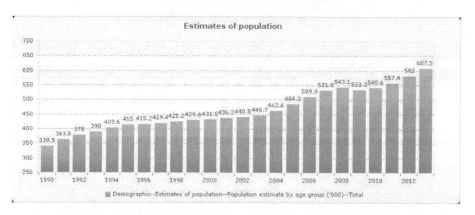

From the chart "the Population in Macau," we can see that with 23 years, the population in Macau has increased from 339,500 in 1990 to 607,500 in 2013.[5] We have to say that the steady growth of population brings a lot of pressure to this small place. Logically, in a general society with no major changes (such as war, nuclear accident or other events), the relationship between the population and the student number is a positive correlation. That means the bigger population is, the bigger student number is. Based on the above assumption, the total number of students with special education needs should be positive associated with the total student number in a positive way

---

3 See official statistics of the DSEC http://www.dsec.gov.mo/default.aspx?noredirect=true; accessed on 1st of September, 2014.

4 See official statistics of the DSEC http://www.dsec.gov.mo/default.aspx?noredirect=true; accessed on 1st of September, 2014.

5 See official statistics of the DSEC http://www.dsec.gov.mo/default.aspx?noredirect=true; accessed on 1st of September, 2014.

as well. With the population increasing, the number of students with special education needs will not be smaller than it used to be. Macau is a normal society with no major changes, which means it can be predicted that: with a bigger population, the total amount of student number will be bigger, and the group of students needing special education and related services will be larger. Normally, the relationship between the population of an area and the number of students with special education needs of the same area is proportional. On the other hand, when the special education students' group grows larger, with no doubt, the demand of resource allocation from the education system will increase as well. Meanwhile, facing the education system resource allocation issue, legislations and regulations will be needed to guide the special education into a positive development and to balance the social resource.

Leaving this special education resource allocation aside, in order to solve the problem of "overcrowded living" in Macau, the government takes reclamation as a solution to reduce the population density. The society is changing greatly and the economy is in an explosive growth in Macau. The land area of Macau almost doubled in the past 23 years from 17.4 km² in 1990 to 30.3 km² in 2013.[6]

---

6   See official statistics of the DSEC http://www.dsec.gov.mo/default.aspx?noredirect=true; accessed on 1st of September, 2014.

3.1   The Total Area of Macau[7]

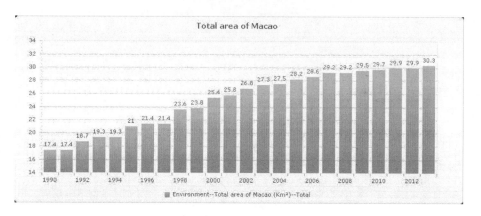

The original land area is limited, and the total land area is increasing so rapidly with the implementation of reclamation by the Macau government. Comparing with other areas in the world, Macau and the Netherlands are two typical examples for the cases relying on the reclamation to adjust the development of economy and society. It is interesting to see that with the population increasing, the total land area is increasing as well in such a rapid way. Bigger land area can bring more space to society development, meanwhile, it's also easier to find places to build schools or the related intuitions. The related facilities of education can be built, which is a good sign for the society and the education system.

Certainly, the population density is not sky high with ongoing reclamation expansion, even the population is climbing.

---

7 See official statistics of the DSEC http://www.dsec.gov.mo/default.aspx?noredirect=true; accessed on 1st of September, 2014.

3.1   The Population Density of Macau[8]

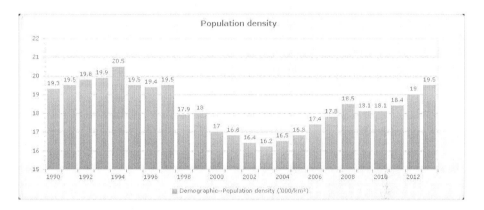

Although the population density had its ups and downs, we can see in the chart of "the Population Density of Macau" that there was not too much difference between the population density in 1990 and 2013.

Simply put, the changing population, the land area and population density are some of the basic elements that can imply the development of the society. There is no doubt that if special education is influenced by these basic elements, the legislation of special education should be improved to better adapt to the practice, to better support the education right and for a better regulation of special education into a positive development. Logically, the increase of population means the total amount of students with special education needs would increase as well. The increasing land area means there is idle land for school building which can keep up with the increasing rate of student number. The population density can at least tell us that, normally, with the society developing, the resource for each student is not decreasing although the population is bigger during the development of society.

---

8   See official statistics of the DSEC http://www.dsec.gov.mo/default.aspx?noredirect=true; accessed on 1st of September, 2014.

All in all, the above three elements may not be the key influencing factors to special education comparing with the proportion of education funds or the influence of legal bias, but they are the basic indicators for us to have an overall picture of the society in Macau, so that we can have a clearer understanding of how a specific phenomenon happens or changes, like the changes of special education. Subsequently, the legislation of special education to better regulate the changes of special education is at the corner.

3.2　The relevant data of special education in Macau

There are a few key statistics representing the special education, and the following data may give us a clearer image on special education in Macau.

In the 2011 Results of Census of Macau, around 11,141 people out of the total population were disabled.[9] It was not a small group in such a small area. Everyone had the equal opportunity to receive education under the law; it was not an easy job to provide appropriate special education to around 11 thousand people[10] in a society with just more than 552 thousand populations.[11] The percentage of disabilities was 1.834%. Every 100 people had 1.8 people with disabilities. As the development goes by, how to provide this group with proper education and related services has become an inevitable topic for the society to discuss.

According to the academic data, there were 7,901 people with a special

---

9　See official statistics of the DSEC ed., RESULTS OF THE CENSUS 2011 (人口普查), Macau: DSEC (04/2012), p21.

10 See official statistics of the DSEC ed., RESULTS OF THE CENSUS 2011 (人口普查), Macau: DSEC (04/2012), p21.

11 See official statistics of the DSEC ed., RESULTS OF THE CENSUS 2011 (人口普查), Macau: DSEC (04/2012), p109.

educational degree of primary school or lower than primary school,[12] the ratio was 71.1% in the total population of the disabled; the percentage of the disabled with an education degree of middle school was 12.9% in the total population of the disabled; the percentage of the disabled with an education degree of high school was 9.0% in the total population of the disabled; and the percentage of the disabled with an education degree of higher education was only 3.7% in the total population of the disabled.[13] The proportion of the disabled with an education degree of primary school or under primary school was very big and was in the majority. That meant a lot of the people with disabilities were having a very low education or barely had any education at all. It made them hard to get into the society and made them the isolated group from the world. Fortunately, the situation has been changing and getting better in Macau.

Special education in Macau keeps a stable pace in developing, and legislative lobbying plays an indispensable role in this issue. Chapter Two has already shown us how special education and the related special education law changed. The legal system has changed in a tremendous way since the government of the People's Republic of China resumed its sovereignty over Macau on December 20th, 1999. Macau has the Law No.9/2006 and the Decree Law No.33/96/M to regulate special education. If we want to talk about the law of special education in Macau, we should get familiar with the general situation of special education in Macau so that we can acknowledge how many people are directly influenced by the law of special education.

---

[12] See official statistics of the DSEC ed., RESULTS OF THE CENSUS 2011 (人口普查), Macau: DSEC (04/2012), p21.

[13] See official statistics of the DSEC ed., RESULTS OF THE CENSUS 2011 (人口普查), Macau: DSEC (04/2012), p21.

3.2.1 The general details of special education in Macau

According to the latest Statistics in 2012 from Documentation and Information Centre of the Statistics and Census Service (the DSEC), there were nine special schools/institutions in Macau with 113 special education teachers.[14] For a better understanding of the situation, we can go through the following charts:

3.2.1   The Number of Special Education Schools/Institutions in Macau[15]

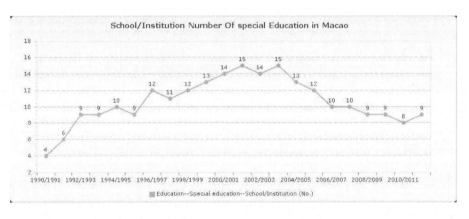

14 See official statistics of the DSEC http://www.dsec.gov.mo/default.aspx?noredirect=true; accessed on 1st of September, 2014.

15 See official statistics of the DSEC http://www.dsec.gov.mo/default.aspx?noredirect=true; accessed on 1st of September, 2014.

3.2.1   The Number of Special Education Teachers in Macau[16]

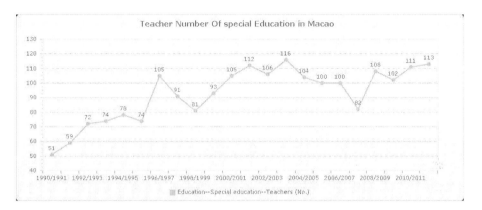

With a few volatility waves, the number of special education teachers was increasing. We can see from the chart of "The Number of Special Education Teachers in Macau" that although the number of special education teachers had its ups and downs, the number was on a rising trend, but the teachers' number was doubled in the past 22 years. Under the education system in Macau, it is the government to fund most of the schools in Macau, and the schools pay for the teachers' salary; in other words, the government funds the most part of the teachers' salary. With more teachers devoting into special education and the average salary increasing, local government is making a bigger appropriation to support the teachers' salary to keep the educational system functional. In terms of recruitment of special education teachers, there are increasing recourse allocation pointing to it by the government, which is a very essential factor influencing the development of special education in Macau.

---

16 See official statistics of the DSEC http://www.dsec.gov.mo/default.aspx?noredirect=true; accessed on 1st of September, 2014.

3.2.1 The Student Enrolled Number of Special Education in Macau[17]

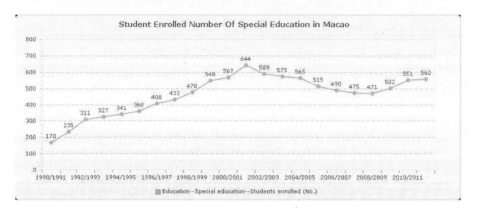

3.2.1 The Student Graduated Number of Special Education in Macau[18]

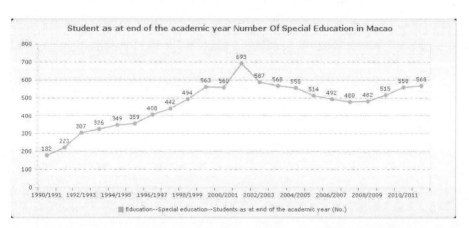

The above two chats show us that the student number of special education was overall raising in Macau. The rates of enrollment and finish of the academic year were basically flat. The total need for special education is

---

[17] See official statistics of the DSEC http://www.dsec.gov.mo/default.aspx?noredirect=true; accessed on 1st of September, 2014.

[18] See official statistics of the DSEC http://www.dsec.gov.mo/default.aspx?noredirect=true; accessed on 1st of September, 2014.

climbing due to the growing population. It fits the trend of student number of special education. The above trends[19] show that, more and more professionals dedicate the special education career when more students need special education. The increasing population in Macau brings more demands to the society, and with the population growing, the society can afford more teachers for the special education system. Most of the schools (both private and public) and institutions are funded by the government, which on the other side, with more teachers teaching special education; the government is allocating more funds on special education.

3.2.2 The specific details of special education in Macau

With the above analysis of the general details of special education, we may have a better overview of the special education in Macau. After that, we can dig deeper and see some detailed statistics concerning special education in Macau.

Before we go through the subsequent data below, we should be clear about two points: firstly, rather than implementing traditional pull-out settings of special education, nowadays in Macau, special education is mainly implemented in inclusive education in regular schools (both public schools and private schools). The reason to implement inclusive education instead of traditional pull-out setting of special education is that, based on the worldwide studies, the outcome of combined service models (partial inclusive education) of special education is better than pull-out only (traditional pull-out settings of

---

19 The trends include the charts of "3.2.1 The Number of Special Education Schools/Institutions in Macau", "3.2.1 The Number of Special Education Teachers in Macau", "3.2.1 The Student Enrolled Number of Special Education in Macau" and "3.2.1 The Student Graduated Number of Special Education in Macau".

special education).[20] There are three ways to implement special education: inclusive education class, small special education class and special education class. Here is the data of the implementation of these ways:

3.2.2 The Details of Students with Special Education Needs from Different Types of Schools[21]

Schoo Types / Placemen Types	Public School	Private School	Total Number
Inclusive Education Class	9	28	37
Small Class of Special Education	2	-	2
Special Education Class	5	4	9

Secondly, after we know the three ways of implementing special education in Macau, we may realize from the inclusive education class, there are regular students and inclusive students studying in the same class.

---

[20] Marston Douglas "A comparison of inclusion only, pull-out only, and combined service models for students with mild disabilities", The Journal of Special Education, Vol.30 Issue2, 1996, pp121-132.

[21] See official statistics of DSEJ http://portal.dsej.gov.mo/webdsejspace/internet/Inter_main_page.jsp#; accessed on 10th of September, 2014; those materials are rearranged and translated by the author.

3.2.2   The Details of Students with Special Education Needs[22]

Types Academic Year	Public School		Private School		Total
	Special education students	Inclusive education students	Special education students	Inclusive education students	
2004/2005 academic year	315	148	215	9	687
2005/2006 academic year	297	151	211	15	674
2006/2007 academic year	285	161	205	50	701
2007/2008 academic year	262	181	213	83	739
2008/2009 academic year	262	200	209	133	804
2009/2010 academic year	262	190	240	182	874
2010/2011 academic year	272	189	279	237	977
2011/2012 academic year	283	170	277	314	1044
2012/2013 academic year	290	131	292	385	1098
2013/2014 academic year	313	168	299	524	1304

The data of the forms "the Details of Students with Special Education Needs from Different Types of Schools" and "the Details of Students with Special Education Needs" were collected from the official website of the DSEJ. Both special education students and inclusive education students are regulated by the Law No.9/2006 and the Decree Law No.33/96/M. The sources have been updated since November 2013.

We can see the total number of students with special education needs is mounting year after year. After nine years the total number of special

---

22 See official statistics of DSEJ http://www.dsej.gov.mo/cappee/cappee08/se/se5.html; accessed on 10th of September, 2014; the materials are rearranged and translated by the author.

education students almost doubled from the beginning with 687 special education students in 2004/2005 academic year (see the form of "the Details of Students with Special Education Needs") to 1304 special education students in 2013/2014 academic year (see the form of "the Details of Students with Special Education Needs"). This was a fast growing trend. The trend fits our assumption of "The positive correlation between population and the number of students with special education needs under the circumstance of no major changes happened in the society" in "Chapter Three 3.1 the environmental element and the population".

In the form of "the Details of Students with Special Education Needs", firstly, within almost a decade from 2004/2005 academic year to 2013/2014 academic year, the number of special education students did not change a lot both in public schools from 315 to 313 and private schools from 215 to 299.[23] The numbers were stable and barely waved. The situation of special education students was in a saturated position. "The number for special education schools to receive" might be on par with "the number for special education schools can receive". The supply and demand were equal for each other in the case of special education student. However, and secondly, the interaction between special education and special education law was very clear. The Law No.9/2006 was to take effect in 2006. We can see an obvious difference from the number of inclusive education students. Especially in private schools, the number of inclusive education students in 2013/2014 academic year was 524, which increased 58.2 times from nine inclusive education students in the earlier 2004/2005 academic year.[24] This growth was not a usual phenomenon

---

23 See official statistics of DSEJ http://www.dsej.gov.mo/cappee/cappee08/se/se5.html; accessed on 10th of September, 2014; the materials are rearranged and translated by the author.

24 See official statistics of DSEJ http://www.dsej.gov.mo/cappee/cappee08/se/se5.html; accessed on 10th of September, 2014; the materials are rearranged and translated by the author.

without the influence of the external force. We can see the turning point was in 2006/2007 academic year. The number of inclusive education students in private school had tripled from only 15 students in 2005/2006 academic year to 50 students in 2006/2007 academic year.[25] Constantly, the number went all the way up until 2013/2014 academic year, the number of inclusive education student in private school reached 524 students. What was the reason of the explosive growth? The legislation of the Law No.9/2006 was put into force in 2006. The key reason for explosive growing number of inclusive education students was caused by Paragraph 3 of Article 12 of the Law No.9/2006. It states that special education preferentially develops inclusive education in regular school, it may also take place in the institutions of special education through other forms.[26] The legislation is strongly influencing the development of inclusive education in both public regular schools and private public schools. As the law's preferential development of special education approaches, inclusive education is the first option for the implementation of special education. The demand from the number of students with special education needs acts to the legislation of special education, and legislation reacts on the regulation of special education and the showing of its' influence on the number changing of inclusive education students.

Education is always an important aspect for the government to concern, special education should be included. It can be told from the data that the situation of special education in Macau can be improved. The legislation of special education can play a major role in the development of Macau. We will

---

25 See official statistics of DSEJ http://www.dsej.gov.mo/cappee/cappee08/se/se5.html; accessed on 10th of September, 2014; the materials are rearranged and translated by the author.

26 The Law Number 9/2006 (the Macau Fundamental Law of Non-Tertiary Education System), Article 12; the articles are in Chinese version and Portuguese version; the articles in English version are translated by the author.

talk about the legal solution for the improvement of special education in Macau in the following chapter.

Chapter Four
The Problems Relating to Individuals of
Special Education in the Legal System

The main existing laws relating to special education in Macau are the Law No.9/2006 and the Decree Law No.33/96/M. The promulgation of the Decree Law No.33/96/M has promoted the development of special education in a remarkable manner, and has made the education of Macau to step into a new level. However, as time goes by, the Decree Law No.33/96/M did not harmonize for the development of special education in Macau any more. Not only just a few articles are not applicable, albeit the Decree Law No.33/96/M itself is also not practical and operational enough for the implementation of the need for students with special education needs. Even the Law No.9/2006 regulates some content of special education, there is only one article.[1] Article 12 of the Law No.9/2006 is an general article to special education, and under the circumstance of Article 54 of the Law No.9/2006,[2] the main guidance of special education in the legal system is still the Decree Law No.33/96/M.

The following paragraphs will mainly talk about the defects in the legal system in Macau. We will start from the rights and obligations of the people who are involved in special educational system. During the whole process of

---

[1] The Law No.9/2006 (the Macau Fundamental Law of Non-Tertiary Education System), Article 12.

[2] The Law No.9/2006 (the Macau Fundamental Law of Non-Tertiary Education System), Article 54 regulates that those laws supplementing the Law No.11/91/M which do not counteract Law No.9/2006 (the Macau Fundamental Law of Non-Tertiary Education System), the remain in force until the new complementary law put into force.

implementation of special education, some of the personnel are directly related to it. Those people are the students, parents, educators, and other related service providers.

4.1 The students with special education needs of special education in the legal system

Normally, the restricted special education is the education provided to the students with physical and psychological limitations.[3] The special education with a broader sense is the education provided to those students who cannot receive the appropriate education corresponded with the characteristics in the regular education system.[4] Thus, there are two kinds of classifications for students with special education. One is restricted only for the students with physical and psychological limitations, such as the handicapped people.[5] The other one is in a broader sense including not only the students with physical and psychological limitations but also students with born disabilities.[6] Macau belongs to the latter one.

In Macau, both the Law No.9/2006 and the Decree Law No.33/96/M have the articles to regulate the students with physical and psychological limitations and students with born disabilities. Based on the Law No.9/2006, both students with physical and born disabilities and psychological limited students are

---

3 Ruan Bangqiu, "Macau Special Education: Review and Hope", Administration, Vol.21 issue79 No.1, 2008, pp81-104.

4 Ruan Bangqiu, "Macau Special Education: Review and Hope", Administration, Vol.21 issue79 No.1, 2008, pp81-104.

5 Like the students in the People with Disabilities Education Ordinance in Chinese (《中華人民共和國殘疾人教育條例》).

6 Like the students in Paragraph 2 of Article 12 of the Law No.9/2006 (the Macau Fundamental Law of Non-Tertiary Education System).

included in the categorization of the students with special education needs[7]
that we discuss in the thesis. The related statutes of classification of special
education students are as follows:

4.1   The Classification of Students with Special Education Needs[8]

Law	Article	Content
The Decree Law No.33/96/M (the Macau Decree Law of Special Education System)	Article 1 (Scope of application)	This Law applies to students with temporary or permanent need of special education, which attending integrated educational institutions in the educational system.
	Paragraph 1 of Article 2 (Guiding principles)	The students with special educational needs which arising from the characteristics in physical, sensory, mental, emotional, and social aspects, can receive special education; it requires that the educational process respects these differences in order to promote their educational success and promote their social integration.
The Law No.9/2006 (the Macau Fundamental Law	Paragraph 2 of Article 12 (Special education)	The special education recipients are evaluated by the relevant public services department or the entities

---

7   The Law No.9/2006 (the Macau Fundamental Law of Non-Tertiary Education System), Article 12.

8   The Decree Law No.33/96/M (the Macau Decree Law of Special Education System); the Law No.9/2006 (the Macau Fundamental Law of Non-Tertiary Education System); the articles are in Chinese version and Portuguese version; the articles in English version are translated by the author.

Law	Article	Content
of Non-Tertiary Education System)		identified by the responsible depart-ment, those special education recipients are including students with born disabilities and those with physical and psychological limitations.

We cannot identify students with what kind of disabilities or what kind of gifts through the relevant provision in the Law No.9/2006, because the regulation is too general. The situation of the students' identification is the same in the Decree Law No.33/96/M. Actually, those articles in the form above are just repeatedly saying that, if you are a student with special education needs, you can have the right to receive special education and related service. The articles fail to give the standards or even fail to give the classifications for students, parents or schools to refer to. This kind of law is not operable enough to deal with the implementation of special education and it makes the articles vague. There are no clear and detailed reference and standards regarding to the students' disabilities and talents for us to distinguish in the articles. However, we can tell from Paragraph 2 of Article 12 of the Law No.9/2006 that at least there are two kinds of students with special education needs that are eligible to the legal categorization to receive special education and related services: the students with physical and psychological limitations and students with born disabilities.[9]

---

[9] The Law No.9/2006 (the Macau Fundamental Law of Non-Tertiary Education System), Paragraph 2 of Article 12.

4.1.1 The students with physical and psychological limitations

Who is under the protection from the related special education law in Macau? Paragraph 2 of Article 12 of the Law No.9/2006 (the Macau Fundamental Law of Non-Tertiary Education System) says "special education recipients include students with born disabilities and those with physical and psychological limitations".[10] No more details are written in the paragraph, so we have to turn to the Decree Law No.33/96/M A student must fit into the classification, so that he/she can receive special education and related services. We can see Paragraph 1 of Article 2 of the Decree Law No.33/96/M which says, the students with special educational needs arising from the characteristics of physical, sensory, mental, emotional, and social can receive special education.[11] If you want to use this article to settle the issue of classification of special education students, you will find it not specific enough to tackle your problem: it is not an operable article for the legal implementation.

The article does not scientifically classify those physical and psychological limitations in a systematic way, which makes it vague and general and hard to put into enforcement. For example, if a student has attention deficit hyperactivity disorder (ADHD), can he/she receive special education according to the classification of Paragraph 2 of Article 12 of the Law No.9/2006 or Paragraph 1 of Article 2 of the Decree Law No.33/96/M? On the other hand, what about a student with learning disabilities? Or what if a

---

10 The Law No.9/2006 (the Macau Fundamental Law of Non-Tertiary Education System), Paragraph 2 of Article 12.

11 The Decree Law No.33/96/M (the Macau Decree Law of Special Education System), Article 2; the articles are in Chinese version and Portuguese version; the articles in English version are translated by the author.

student has no friend, is that a social disorder for him/her? Even more, can he/she receive special education under the law based on this situation? Simply put, the Decree Law No.33/96/M does not give us a clear classification of who can or cannot receive special education and related services because "the characteristics of physical, sensory, mental, emotional, and social" [12] are sorts of human functional generality, nor a categorization of standard for students with special education needs, and the inappropriate classification of special education students will influence the implementation of special education.

With the worldwide trend of the special education development, some other areas do a good job to protect the education right for the students with special education needs by the establishment of an efficient and implementable legal system. The beginning to establish an efficient and implementable legal system is to scientifically categorize the characteristics of the special education students. Due to the Decree Law No.33/96/M does not give us enough details on the categorization of special education students. Through the regulation of this issue in other areas may give us the answer to what kind of students shall be protected under the special education law.

4.1.1.1 The students with physical and psychological limitations in the United States of America

For further understanding, the thesis will examine the law of special education in other countries. Firstly, the United States of America has a comprehensive legal system and provides well-developed special education for its people. Its regulation of special education is comprehensive and advanced around the world. We can go through the related special education law in the United States of America as an example to have a better understanding about

---

12 The Decree Law No.33/96/M (the Macau Decree Law of Special Education System), Article 2.

who are eligible under the protection of special education law.

The United States of America has the following laws that relate to special education:

a. Section 504 of the Rehabilitation Act.

b. The Individuals with Disabilities Education Act.

Normally, to be eligible for to the protection under those laws, an individual must meet the definition of the regulations about the categorization for individuals with special education needs.

The definition of a person with a disability in section 504 in the United States of America is as the following content:

> *Any person who (i) has a physical or metal impairment which substantially limits one of more if such person's major life activities, (ii) has a record of such an impairment, or (iii) is regarded as having such an impairment.*[13]

The definition of a child with a disability of the individuals with disabilities education act is:

> *Child with a disability means a child evaluated in accordance with the law as those having*[14] *13 categories: Mental retardation; Hearing impairment (including deafness); Speech or language impairment; Visual impairment (including blindness); Serious emotional disturbance (referred to in this part as "emotional disturbance"); Orthopedic impairment; Autism; Traumatic brain injury; Other health impairment; Specific learning disability; Deaf-*

---

[13] 34 C.F.R Section 300.8 (c) (4).

[14] 20 U.S.C. Section 1401 (3); 34 C.R.F Section 300.8.

blindness; Multiple disabilities and who, by reason thereof, needs special education and related services.

In the Individuals with Disabilities Education Act, the categorization of the special education students is very detailed, including a variety of physical and psychological limitations. As the definition is direct and operable, no legal inference is needed in this categorization, those students with special education needs can be applied with special education and related services once they are eligible for the categorization of the Individuals with Disabilities Education Act.

4.1.1.2 The students with physical and psychological limitations in Taiwan

Comparing with Macau, the United States of America is a country with a different legal system. A more similar legal system may give us a more direct idea of the appropriate classification of students with physical and psychological limitations in legislation. Taiwan is an area having many similarities with Macau in all aspects, such as the culture and the social background. We may get a deeper understanding of what is an appropriate classification in legislation of the students with physical and psychological limitations through a comparison of the relevant regulation between Taiwan and Macau.

Taiwan has the following regulations related with special education:

a. The Taiwan Special Education Law.

b. The Taiwan Enforcement Rules of the Special Education Act.

They are the major laws guiding the implementation of special education in Taiwan. Not all the students with disabilities are covered by the special education law. To be eligible for the protection under the Taiwan Special

Education Law, a student must fit into the definition of a student with disability under the law.

The definition of a student with disabilities of the Taiwan Special Education Law regulates by Article 3:

Disabilities meant in the Act are referred to as physiological or psychological disorders, assessed and diagnosed by professionals to be in need of special education and related services, and categorized as13 categories: Intellectual Disabilities; Visual Impairments; Hearing Impairments; Communication Disorders; Physical Impairments; Cerebral Palsy; Health Impairments; Severe Emotional Disorders; Learning Disabilities; Severe/Multiple Impairments; Autism; Developmental Delays and Other Disabilities.

We can see that the categorization of the Taiwan Special Education Law is very familiar with the Individuals with Disabilities Education Act. The categorization systematically regulates the physical and psychological limitations for those students to receive special education and related services.

4.1.1.3   The comparison of the categorization of students with physical and psychological limitations in the United States of America, Taiwan and Macau

The regulations of the categorizations in the United States of America and Taiwan are operational in practice. The detailed categorizations of the physical and psychological limitations can help people to easily define the eligibility of the student in the legal aspect. However, Macau regulate this area in a more general way, we can see the details in the following form:

4.1.1.3 The Categorization of Students with Special Education Needs in the Laws of the United States of America, Taiwan and Macau[15]

Area	Law	The definition of a student with disability under the law
The United States of America	The Individuals with Disabilities Education Act	A. *Mental retardation.* B. *Hearing impairment (including deafness),* C. *Speech or language impairment,* D. *Visual impairment (including blindness),* E. *Serious emotional disturbance (referred to in this part as "emotional disturbance"),* F. *Orthopedic impairment,* G. *Autism,* H. *Traumatic brain injury,* I. *Other health impairment,* J. *Specific learning disability,* K. *Deaf-blindness,* L. *Multiple disabilities,* M. *Who, by reason thereof, needs special education and related services*
Taiwan	The Taiwan Special Education Law	A. *Intellectual Disabilities.* B. *Visual Impairments.* C. *Hearing Impairments.* D. *Communication Disorders.* E. *Physical Impairments.* F. *Cerebral Palsy.*

---

[15] The form includes the regulation of the categorization in the Individuals with Disabilities Education Act, the Taiwan Special Education Law and the Decree Law No.33/96/M (the Macau Decree Law of Special Education System); the materials are rearranged and translated by the author.

Area	Law	The definition of a student with disability under the law
		G. *Health Impairments.*
		H. *Severe Emotional Disorders.*
		I. *Learning Disabilities.*
		J. *Severe/Multiple Impairments.*
		K. *Autism.*
		L. *Developmental Delays.*
		M. *Other Disabilities*
Macau	The Decree Law No.33/96/M (the Macau Decree Law of Special Education System)	*Physical, sensory, mental, emotional and social order*

From the above form, we can find the defect about the classification of students with disabilities in the Decree Law No.33/96/M clearly. The classifications of students with physical and psychological limitations in the U.S. and Taiwan are operable enough that you can justify and determine if a student is qualified to receive special education and related services or not. In addition to the categories of the students with physical and psychological limitations, both legal systems in the U.S. and Taiwan have similar regulations: the option M "the other disabilities".[16] This option is a safe clause and may give the maximum protection to the educational rights for students.

However, unlike the applicable regulations in the Individuals with Disabilities Education Act or the Taiwan Special Education Law, the Decree Law No.33/96/M does not elaborate too many details in the article of the

---

16 The Individuals with Disabilities Education Act, the Taiwan Special Education Law and the Decree Law No.33/96/M (the Macau Decree Law of Special Education System).

classification. It only says that the students with special education needs arising from the characteristics of physical, sensory, mental, emotional and social can receive special education.[17] Both the U.S. and Taiwan have the categories of disabilities. Each category has its own specific requirements to meet so that a student could be eligible to receive special education and related services. The definition about who can receive special education in the Decree Law No.33/96/M is too broad to enforce. It may be a medical issue to define the physical and psychological limitation of an individual, and the legislation is supposed to give us a direction to tell one from the others. Like the Individuals with Disabilities Education Act and the Taiwan Special Education Law, both of them are able to idetify the laws that protect each individual's disabilities, while the Decree Law No.33/96/M fails to do this.

4.1.2 Students with born disabilities

The child must require special education services for better development. due to his/her disabilities. The Law No.9/2006, Paragraph 2 of Article 12 stipulates that students with born disabilities can receive special education. But the categorization of students with born disabilities remains uncertain in the article. So we turn to the specific special education law: the Decree Law No.33/96/M to seek the answer. As we can see from the articles in the Decree Law No.33/96/M, students with born disabilities are wrongly classified as well. Actually, no content of the classification of students with born disabilities is written in it, Paragraph 1 of Article 17 simply says: students with born disabilities should take the professional evaluation.[18]

Looking back upon the history about the development of special

---

17 The Decree Law No.33/96/M (the Macau Decree Law of Special Education System), Article 2.
18 The Decree Law No.33/96/M (the Macau Decree Law of Special Education System), Article 17.

education, we may find out that the reason of its beginning goes to the demand of talents' cultivation.[19] The talents play an important role in the development of society, which highlights the significance to scientifically cultivate students with born disabilities.

Per the discussion in the previous chapter, the Decree Law No.33/96/M doesn't appropriately categorize the students with physical and psychological limitations. The categorization of students with born disabilities is under the same circumstance. The Decree Law No.33/96/M became effective in 1996. The public was not familiar with the concept of students with born disabilities and it was rather strange for people to understand at that time. However, the legislator of special education law foresaw the development of special education and regulated the related legal matters of students with born disabilities in Article 17 of the Decree Law No.33/96/M.

Article 17 of the Decree Law No.33/96/M has statement about the evaluation of students with born disabilities, saying that students with born disabilities are subject to special evaluation, whenever deemed necessary, at the request of the teacher or the class teacher, seeking enrichment or accelerated learning of curriculum content, the class teacher should inform the student and the parent/guardian of the outcome of learning achievement within the Individualized Education Plan and Educational Activities Program.[20]

As time passed by, the Law No.9/2006 renewed some content about students with born disabilities. We can see Paragraph 2 of Article 12 in he Law No.9/2006 describes that students with born disabilities and those students

19 Hsiu-Chi Guo, "Discussion on the Strategies for the Gifted Education of Taiwan", School Administration Research Association, R.O.C. Bimonthly Newsletter of School Administration Research Association (SARA), September 2009, pp154-175.

20 The Decree Law No.33/96/M (the Macau Decree Law of Special Education System), Article 17; the articles are in Chinese version and Portuguese version; the articles in English version are translated by the author.

with physical and psychological limitations can receive special education and related services[21]. This article put students with born disabilities in the students' categorization of who can receive special education and related services. One interesting thing in this Law is, this time, the legislator puts students with born disabilities in front of the students with physical and psychological limitations, which means the Law No.9/2006 really pays attention to improve the legal status of students with born disabilities.

4.2 The parents of special education in the legal system

Individuals under the age of 18 in Macau are minors.[22] They are generally presumed as legally incompetent under the law to make agreements or their decisions. Both the Law No.9/2006 and the Decree Law No.33/96/M in Macau aim to provide proper special education to those students with special education needs.[23] The student's preference is a valuable consideration; however, most of the decisions are made by their parents. Parental right in this issue is indispensable and should be written down in law. However, as a general article, Article 12 of the Law No.9/2006 does not regulate the parental right in detail. We may turn to the Decree Law No.33/96/M to take a deeper understanding of the regulation of parental right in special education.

---

[21] The Law number 9/2006 (the Macau Fundamental Law of Non-Tertiary Education System), Paragraph 2 of Article 12.

[22] The Macau Civil Code, Article 111.

[23] The Decree Law No.33/96/M (the Macau Decree Law of Special Education System), Article 2; the Law number 9/2006 (the Macau Fundamental Law of Non-Tertiary Education System), Article 12.

4.2.1 The overview of the parental rights in the Decree Law No.33/96/M

Parents or guardians are an essential component to the effectiveness in the reality during the whole process of the implementation of special education. Parents or guardians will be consulted constantly for the student's background and situation by teachers, schools, or the related institutions (such as the medical institute, the CPPSSE and so on).

In the Decree Law No.33/96/M, Article 16 clearly states the right for the consent of parent/guardian. Paragraph 1 of Article 16 says that before evaluating students with special education needs, it is required to obtain the consent of their parents.[24] Second paragraph states that it is necessary for the parents to acknowledge the Individualized Education Plan and Educational Activities Program.[25] Putting aside from the rationality of the attitude on different parental rights with evaluation and Individualized Education Plan and Educational Activities Program, the law is reasonable and is paying attention to the protection of the parental rights on special education issues.

4.2.2 The defects of the parental rights in the Decree Law No.33/96/M

The law regulates the parental right on approving the evaluation of the student and the parental right on acknowledging the Individualized Education Plan (Individualized Education Plan is the educational program decided for a specific student with special education needs).[26] The intention of those

---

24 The Decree Law No.33/96/M (the Macau Decree Law of Special Education System), Article 16.

25 The Decree Law No.33/96/M (the Macau Decree Law of Special Education System), Article 16.

26 The Individualized Education Plan will be discussed in chapter five.

provisions is that the person who is legally responsible for the student shall be the person responsible for making special educational and the related decisions during the processes of the implementation of his/her child's special education. Not only because the parents are familiar with his/her own child, but also they can ensure the attendance of the student to the related activities (such as attending to school, doing the evaluation and receiving medical treatment and so on) which they ought to participate in.

4.2.2.1 The missing regulation of the parental right on placement

The Decree Law No.33/96/M regulates the rights for parent/guardian on the processes of student's evaluation and the Individualized Education Plan and the Educational Activities Program.[27] However, the law fails to regulate the parental right on the issue about the placement of the students with special education needs. It is the same with the identification, evaluation and development of Individualized Education Plan, placement of the student is one of the processes of the implementation of the special education as well. In reality, when deciding the placement of special education students, the parents or the guardians are the first to be asked for consent on doing so. Only the parents or guardians can ensure student's attendance in school in each family. Without the legislation of the parental consent or acknowledgement of the student's placement, the related authorized institutes (schools or the CPPSSE) can make the decision of the placement that being considered as the best option for the academic and future development for the child without consultation from parents. Parental consent would be neglected if no law regulates it. However, in all the cases concerning special education decision,

---

27 The Educational Activities Program will be discussed in chapter five.

parent's opinions count. The authorized institute might ignore or neglect the parent's circumstance and make some placement decisions for the students with special education needs that parents cannot cooperate or coordinate. For example: the authorized institute decides by placing the student in the school which is the most qualified one to provide special education and related services based on the student's physical and psychological conditions. Regardless, the parents find out that the school is too far away from their living place, no shuttle bus is available for daily transportation, and it is not even a boarding school. Although the school is the best choice for the student; the parents may not be capable enough to transport the child to and from school in routine. Because the law does not regulate the parental right of placement, it is possible that the parent would be put into this negative legal situation. The missing regulation of the parental right of student's placement will expose the parent/guardian to a situation that parent/guardian has no voice on the placement of their children. The outcome would escalate into the situation where the parents refuse to take the child to the designated school. The related institute may take the disagreement of the parent as an unreasonable action and may refuse to remake the decision. Then the child's education right would be endangered.

4.2.2.2 The dispute between the parental consent and authorized decision

When the law regulates the parental rights for the evaluation, the Individualized Education Plan and the Educational Activities Program, the legislator must consider the situation that parents/guardians are is the most responsible and thoughtful individual for the child. Under some circumstances, not every case is as pleased as we thought. Sometimes there is disagreement over the issue of evaluation because the parent/guardian does not fulfill the parental obligation to take enough care of their child, or because the disagreement of the student occurs between the parent/guardian and the related authorized institute. It is very likely that both sides (the parent/guardian and the related authorized institute) think what they do is for the best interest of the child, the authorized institute can be much more considerable than the parent/guardian. But the law regulates that some processes of the implementation of special education have to have the parental consent.[28] Without the consent of the parent/guardian, the authorized institute cannot evaluate the student and implement special education for the student even if the student is the one with special education needs.

If the parent/guardian refuses to agree with the evaluation decision from the related authorized institute, the child may risk being deprived of his/her education right, because it means the student may at risk of losing the chance to receive proper education. In this case, because the law gives the right to parent/guardian over the agreement of the evaluation of the students with special education needs, once the student is considered as a child who may have to be evaluated by the authorized institute, a dispute between the parents and the authorized institute will arise when the parents/guardians do not give their consent over the decision.

We should not conjecture the reason of the parent's refusal to consent on evaluation. The law gives parent/guardian the right to refuse the evaluation; this right is discretionary for the parent/guardian based on goodwill. What if the parent/guardian does not participate in the process of the implementation of special education, or interferes with the refusal to consent to the evaluation and further jeopardizes the benefit of the student's education right? For this similar situation in the U.S., the amendment of IDEA gives the solution on this

---

[28] The Decree Law No.33/96/M (the Macau Decree Law of Special Education System), Article 16.

issue. In the U.S., under the IDEA, if the parent/guardian does not agree with the evaluation for the child, the school may choose to try to override the parent's refusal of consent by going through the dispute resolution process; if the disagreement happens after the evaluation, they can request an independent evaluation as a part of the eligibility decision.[29] This is a good example of enlightenment for solving the same dispute in Macau. However, in the legal system of Macau, this problem remains unsettled.

In any case, there is no doubt that the parents are significant in carrying out the requirements of the Decree Law No.33/96/M. Parental participation requirements include mandatory notification of parent at various stages of the processes and mandates the opportunity for parental participation is available.[30]

4.3 The teachers of special education in the legal system

As a general article, Article 12 of the Law No.9/2006 does not regulate the teachers' right in detail. We may turn to the Decree Law No.33/96/M to take a deeper understand-ing of the regulation of parental right in special education.

To help the special education student to learn and maintain those scientific knowledge and achievements of human discoveries and inventions, special education teachers are the ones who make it happen through educational

---

29 Laura Rothstein & Scott F. Johnson, Special education law, 4th Ed, (Thousand Oaks, CA: Sage Publications, 2010), pp85-103.

30 Laura Rothstein & Scott F. Johnson, Special education law, 4th Ed, (Thousand Oaks, CA: Sage Publications, 2010), p54.

activities.[31] It is very hard to explore the potential of students without a high-quality special education teacher in special education. Without a good teacher, the value to the society of the special education student will be easily wasted. In order to achieve the goal of special education, the related special education law in Macau should regulate teacher's quality, and the educational quality for special education student can be guaranteed, so that the aim of providing "learners with special needs the opportunity to access an education adapted to their physical and psychological, in order to support the social education, the development of potential, the compensation of limitations and the integration into working life"[32] can be achieved.

4.3.1 The provisions of laws concerning special education teacher in Macau

We have discussed the teacher's right and obligation in the related special education law in Macau from the very first beginning, we should know that two different kinds of teachers are involved in special education: 1. the inclusion classroom teachers who teach both regular students and special education students at the same time; 2. teachers who teach students with special education needs in special education school.

Traditionally, the educational methodology and teaching content between these two kinds of teachers are different. One is performing inclusive education which special education students are involved but most of the students are regular students; the other is facing a certain type of special

---

31 Jin Xianghua, "The Research of The Transformation of Development of Korean Special Education", Education Comments, No.5, 2010, pp163-165.

32 The Law number 9/2006 (the Macau Fundamental Law of Non-Tertiary Education System), Paragraph 1 of Article 12; the articles are in Chinese version and Portuguese version; the articles in English version are translated by the author.

education students (like students with visual impairments or intellectual disabilities). However, the Decree Law No.33/96/M does not regulate the requirements for these two kinds of teachers separately. Instead, the Decree Law No.33/96/M just says in Article 18 that the teacher who teaches students with special education needs, should have appropriate relevant training.[33] The training depends on the characteristics of the teaching mode.[34] Before the teacher starts to teach students with special education needs, the teacher has to receive special education training. It is an article which is not very operable during the implementation of special education, because it is not easy to define what level of the special education teacher training is appropriate in the article.

Meanwhile, the Law No.9/2006 regulates the teacher's training as well. Paragraph 5 of Article 12 (special education) states that for improving the development of special education, government should create conditions; one of the conditions is Subparagraph 2: to provide special education training to teachers and other participants.[35] Still, the legal system in Macau does not give us enough detail about the teacher training. It just tells us that special education training for teachers is required.

Nevertheless, this "not operable enough clause of teacher's training situation" may be changed soon under the pressure of the international trend of special education. We can predict the coming legislation of special education in Macau may change with a more detailed classification about the requirements of different types of special education teachers if there is a plan

---

[33] The Decree Law No.33/96/M (the Macau Decree Law of Special Education System), Article 18.

[34] The Decree Law No.33/96/M (the Macau Decree Law of Special Education System), Article 18.

[35] The Law number 9/2006 (the Macau Fundamental Law of Non-Tertiary Education System), Paragraph 5 of Article 12.

to renew the special education law. The trend of inclusive education around the world has been developing for several decades, under this trend, the requests of the special education teachers are much more meticulous than "the teacher in the classes of students with special education needs, should have appropriate relevant training".[36] Further more, the government pays more attention to the special education teachers training and sets up some rules for teachers' qualification in the Law of General Framework of the Teaching Staff of Private Schools in the Non-Tertiary Education (the Law Number 3/2012), which is another approach for forward legislation of the regulation of teachers in special education in Macau. The legislation about the certification requirement of teacher training is way behind than what kind of training the government requests from the teacher to take in reality.

4.3.2 The challenge for teachers under the Decree Law No.33/96/M

Other than parents, teachers are those paying the most attention to the safety and academic achievement of the students. Not all the teachers want to provide special education and related services to students with special education needs which will bring lots of extra work to the teacher during the teaching process. However, if the teachers teach the students with special education needs, the school has to ensure that these teachers are well trained. While facing some situation, the teachers should handle them in the appropriate and adequate way. Besides, the procedures should be clearly elaborated before the implementation of special education. The legal system requires the teachers to have the degree or equivalent qualification in the

---

36 The Decree Law No.33/96/M (the Macau Decree Law of Special Education System), Article 18.

special education area,[37] that includes the component of teacher training or
training qualification recognized by the DSEJ.[38] This concept arose in 1988
by the American scholars. It did not take a long time for teachers to "digest"
this helpful concept.

In recent years, regular teachers and special education teachers work
closer on providing appropriate and adequate special education to students
with special education needs. This makes the situation changing into a much
more collaborative circumstance from isolated work among teachers. The
implementation of the Decree Law No.33/96/M about the trend of inclusion
education gives the teachers a lot of extra pressure especially for the regular
classroom teachers. With so many different special educations needs for
different special education students, the collaboration between regular teachers
and special education teachers is a very good trend for improving the level and
quality of education. Maybe the communication of interrelationship of various
special education teachers is far away from enough, but like the scholars say in
one article: while there have been improvements in collaboration, the trend
goes on is very important.[39]

In order to ensure the teachers to be highly qualified while teaching
students with special education needs, Article 18 of the Decree Law
No.33/96/M is a provision for teachers' training. It ensures that the teachers
who provide special education and related services to students with disabilities
are appropriately and adequately trained. It requires the teachers to join some

---

37 The Decree Law No.33/96/M (the Macau Decree Law of Special Education System), Article
   18.

38 The Law Number 3/2012 (the Macau Law of General Framework of the Teaching Staff of
   Private Schools in the Non-Tertiary Education), Article 10.

39 Jameson J. Matt & Huefner Dixie S, "Highly Qualified special educators and the provision of a
   free appropriate public education to students with disabilities" 35 Journal of law & education,
   Vol.35, Issue 1, January 2006, pp29-50.

professional training which suits the needs for the special education program[40], including the regular classroom teachers with inclusive education students in the class and the special education teachers in the special education schools. Regular classroom teachers have already faced with the increasing professional demands; the unwelcoming of this new and extra stress is understandable. Furthermore, each special education student needs his/her own Individualized Education Plan.[41] By the Law of the General Framework of the Teaching Staff of Private Schools in the Non-Tertiary Education (the Law Number 3/2012), teacher involves in the development of Individualized Education Plan,[42] even the teacher has received help from the CPPSSE during the development of Individualized Education Plan by himself/herself; the teacher has to be the one who implement it. These teachers must have enough knowledge and skills to serve students with special education needs. It may be taken as an unnecessary burden for their teaching life specially teaching in regular class. It causes the concern of the possibility on initial negative reaction of the law by the teachers. As far as the author concerned, this may be the main reason for some schools (most of them are private schools) reject to receive inclusive education students; even most of the teachers are embracing the concept of inclusion education.

In conclusion, the regulation of teacher's duty is not specific enough in the related special education law, and the reality of the implementation of the requirement of the teacher's certification is much more advanced than what

---

[40] The Decree Law No.33/96/M (the Macau Decree Law of Special Education System), Article 18.

[41] The Decree Law No.33/96/M (the Macau Decree Law of Special Education System), Article 12.

[42] The Law Number 3/2012 (the Macau Law of General Framework of the Teaching Staff of Private Schools in the Non-Tertiary Education), Article 8.

Article 18 of the Decree Law No.33/96/M states. It is another essential regulation that falls behind from the actual implementation in special education in Macau. This is still a defect of the Macau legal system and the law of teacher training in special education needs to be renewed.

4.4 The related service providers of special educ-ation in the legal system

To provide special education and related services involves a variety of other individuals within and without the educational system. Except those educators who will have direct contact with the special education students during school life, there are other individuals who will have direct contact with the students with special education needs within and without school life. Those people are the related services providers, and they can make influences to the future development of the students with special education needs. The related services providers are the individuals using profession knowledge to help the students with special education needs to improve themselves for better development in study and in life. Normally, they team up as a group and involve in providing special educational plan and other related supportive services.[43] However, as a general article, Article 12 of the Law No.9/2006 does not regulate the right and obligation of the related services providers. Even worse, no article of the Decree Law No.33/96/M regulates this issue as well. In practice, it is not easy to gather all those individuals together spontaneously; some certain parties or individuals shall take the responsibility to systematically gather them together so that they can work efficiently. On December 21st, 1992, the Decree Law No.81/92/M was issued, and the

---

[43] Laura Rothstein & Scott F. Johnson, Special education law, 4th Ed, (Thousand Oaks, CA: Sage Publications, 2010), pp58-59.

CPPSSE was established based on this legal document. Since then, the CPPSSE was playing the role to gather those related services providers together for a better serving of the students with special education needs.

In Macau, the CPPSSE is the most authoritative institution for special education and related services, and it can be taken as the biggest related services provider for the students with special education needs. It provides the following services:[44]

·To provide services of evaluation and consultation for the students with special education needs;

·To help the students with special education needs of educational placement;

·To provide referral services of the student with medical treatment needs to hospital or other eligible institute;

·To follow up the treatment process of the student with medical treatment needs;

·To provide technical supports for inclusion education and special education of private schools;

·To provide technical supports and training for the school-stay special education working group;

·To conduct workshops and lectures for teachers and parents;

·To improve the development of local special education, including inclusive education and gifted education

·To enrich the information of special education on the internet;

·To develop localized evaluation tools.

---

[44] See official statistics of the DSEJ http://portal.dsej.gov.mo/webdsejspace/internet/Inter_main_ page.jsp#; accessed on 15th of August, 2014; the materials are rearranged and translated by the author.

These services which are provided by the CPPSSE comparatively fit the obligations in Article 17 of the Decree Law No.81/92/M. The above services cover all of the special educational duties of the CPPSSE written in law. Particularly the first point "to provide services of evaluation and consultation for the students with special education needs", this is the essential role for the CPPSSE to be involved in the whole process of the implementation of special education laws. Basically, at the aim of ensuring the right to potential development and ensuring the appropriate educational opportunity for those students with special education needs, there are four points within the services of "evaluation and consultation for the students with special education needs". They are: a. the evaluation of the educational placement; b. evaluation of the treatment; c. professional consultation of special education; d. evaluation of the disabilities.

4.4   The Main Service Details of Evaluation and Consultation[45]

Services	Service details
Evaluation of educational placement	For the student without school placement and being suspected as needing special education or for the student being suspected as needing a transformation of placement
Evaluation of treatment	To help the students diagnosed as individuals having physical dysfunction, language disorder or behavior issue in the medical facilities; or to help and follow up the regular and inclusive students for related treatment after the evaluation of educational placement

---

[45] See official statistics of the DSEJ http://portal.dsej.gov.mo/webdsejspace/internet/Inter_main_
page.jsp#; accessed on 15th of August, 2014; the materials are rearranged and translated by the
author.

Services	Service details
Professional consultation of special education	To help the parents or teachers with solution, improvement or control of the situation after they find out the student has language, learning, behavior, emotional or physical function problems
Evaluation of disabilities	To evaluate the intelligent level of the student who is studying in the formal school in Macau and trying to apply the disability assessment registration certificate.

All the special education and related services that provided by the CPPSSE fit in Article 17 of Decree Law No.81/92/M (the Decree Law of the Current Organizational Structure of the Division of Education and Youth Affairs Bureau):[46]

> g). Define profiles of peculiarity and arrange follow-up plan, adapting it to the educational needs of the student; i). Provide technical and pedagogical supports to the students with special educational needs; j). In conjunction with the Educational Resource Center, organizing the documentation on special education, selecting and disseminating the documentation which can bring interest to educators and families of children and youth with special educational need;

Comparing with the recent implementation and the duties regulated by Article 17 of Decree Law No.81/92/M, there is a big improvement as the CPPSSE fulfilling its' obligation.

---

[46] The Decree Law No.81/92/M (the Decree Law of the Current Organizational Structure of the Division of Education and Youth Affairs Bureau), Article 17; the article is in Chinese version and Portuguese version; the articles in English version are translated by the author.

The Decree Law No.81/92/M does not mention any provisions about the inclusive students. When the Decree Law No.81/92/M was published in 1992, the concept of inclusive education was not very well-known and as popular as nowadays, so the regulation for the legal duty of the CPPSSE in Decree Law No.81/92/M did not mention any obligation for providing any services to inclusive education.

This defect may lead to legal omission of the inclusive students. Once the omission happens, the education right for those inclusive students may be neglected. The missing content of providing special education and related services to the inclusive students and the missing content of providing assistance to inclusive education as an obligation of the CPPSSE are other defects in the recent legal system of the Law No.9/2006 and the Decree Law No.33/96/M, especially the Decree Law No.33/96/M as the specific law for special education. The related service providers are playing the role that not only involved in the evaluation and making of the Individualized Education Plan for the students with special education needs, but also as the implementers of the Decree Law No.33/96/M.

Under most of the circumstances, this team has people with related professional knowledge and degrees so that they can be qualified to objectively achieve the evaluation of students with special education needs, to adequately build up a scientific Individualized Education Plan and to provide other counseling and treatment.

This team is usually made up of the following related services personnel: special education teacher, psychological counselor, occupational therapist, physiotherapist, language therapist, resource teacher and student counselor.[47]

---

[47] See official statistics of the DSEJ http://portal.dsej.gov.mo/webdsejspace/internet/Inter_main_page.jsp#; accessed on 15th of August, 2014. The compositions may be a little different between the team form the Center of Psycho-pedagogical Support and the team from special

Each related service personnel has specific duty to achieve the job so that the content in the Decree Law No.33/96/M can be better implemented and the education right for the students can be protected. Due to no specific law regulates this issue; the duties are set by the CPPSSE.

4.4   The Duty of Related Services Provider[48]

Related service provider	Duty
Special education teacher	· To give study assistance for the students with special education needs depending on the students' characteristics or difficulties; · To provide appropriate special education and related support so that the students can be better developed in academic area; · To formulate the Individualized Education Plan with other team members and parents; · To implement the Individualized Education Plan; · To assess the outcome of the work; · To join in the variety of the educational design and teaching material adaptation
Psychological counselor	· To Provide evaluation and the following up of cognitive ability for the students; · To provide educational lectures for parents and teachers; · To back up the parents and teachers for student issues, especially on the perspectives on student cognitive ability, emotional behavior and family problem

education schools. However, the functions of them are the same: using their professional knowledge to evaluate the students with special education needs objectively and to develop an appropriate individualized educational plan to the student.

[48] See official statistics of the DSEJ http://portal.dsej.gov.mo/webdsejspace/internet/Inter_main_page.jsp#; accessed on 15th of August, 2014; the materials are rearranged and translated by the author.

Related service provider	Duty
Occupational therapist	· To give assistance for the students to improve the coordination of small muscles, cognitive ability, social ability, self-care ability and working skill; · To respond for the evaluation of the above elements; · To design the appropriate individualized or group treatment plan for the students base on the related evaluation; · To give assistance to the students and buy auxiliary appliances for the effectiveness of study and the appropriation of home-based training
Physiotherapist	· To evaluate the development of big muscles of students with special education needs; · To design for appropriate individualized or group treatment plan for the students base on the related evaluation; · To assist students to pick up and buy auxiliary appliances for the effectiveness of study and the appropriation of home-based training and school life
Language therapist	· To give assistance for the student with communication disorders to develop an appropriate and adequate individualized communication way and to help the students to communicate effectively with others in study and in life; · To evaluate the student communicate ability; · To design for appropriate individualized or group treatment plan for the student base on the related evaluation
Student counselor	· To collect information from the parents of the suspected students with special education needs about his/her background, health situation and family status which can help for further and clear acknowledgement of the student development;

Related service provider	Duty
	· To provide related lectures and consultant services for parents; · To follow up the placement situation for the students with special education needs that identified as qualified special education student in the category of the Decree Law No.33/96/M
Resource teacher	· To give study assistance for the students with special education needs in regular class depending on the students' characteristics or difficulties; · To provide appropriate special education and related support so that the students can be better developed in academic area; · To formulate the Individualized Education Plan with other regular teachers and parents; · To implement the Individualized Education Plan; · To assess the outcome of the work; · To join in the variety of de educational design and teaching material adaptation; · To provide professional advice to regular teachers and parents; · To do the publicity work of special education and to broadcast the concept of special education

Occasionally, some of these related service providers provide services for both students with special education needs and regular students. No matter these related services providers are providing services only for students with special education needs or for regular students, it is essential for them to be adequately trained and prepared to work with students.[49] The form above shows us that the division of work is very thoughtful, considerable and well

---

49 Laura Rothstein & Scott F. Johnson, Special education law, 4th Ed, (Thousand Oaks, CA: Sage Publications, 2010), pp58-59.

taken care of most cases of the special education students.

However, with the information that is given by the official website in the above form,[50] there is still something for us to be concerned about.

Again, there is no provision in the Decree Law No.33/96/M regulating the professional background of those related services providers. Different from the Taiwan Special Education Law, it states that all the personnel and administrator responsible for special education services in special education schools and regular schools with special education classes should hire professionals with special education background.[51] The aforementioned special education background is referred to as taking up three or more credit hours of special education courses.[52]

However, d "taking up three or more credit hours of special education courses" remains to be a controversial topic, and this article may be the article which possibly reduces the professionalism of those related services providers.[53] However, we cannot ignore the overall positive influence of this article. Further more, Article 23 of the Taiwan Special Education Law states the relationship between special education and available medical resources about the rehabilitation, training and therapy for special needs students.[54] This article clearly states that special education practices shall be based on the results of professional assessments combined with available medical resources

---

50 The form of "4.4 The Duty for Related Services Provider"; the form is from official statistics See official statistics of the DSEJ http://portal.dsej.gov.mo/webdsejspace/internet/Inter_main_page.jsp#; accessed on 15th of August, 2014; the materials arc rearranged and translated by the author.

51 The Taiwan Special Education Law, Article 7; legislated in 1984, amended in 2013.

52 The Taiwan Special Education Law, Article 7; legislated in 1984, amended in 2013.

53 Hu Yongchong, "The Review of 98-year Edition of Special Education Law", Special Education of Primary School, No.49, June 2010, pp1-9.

54 The Taiwan Special Education Law, Article 23; legislated in 1984, amended in 2013.

for rehabilitation, training and therapy of special needs students.[55] The Taiwan Special Education Law emphases the importance of professionalism in the related services providers, which shows that the obligation of those individuals are important and their qualification shall be regulated when implementing any process of special education.

In Macau, there isn't any article that regulates the qualification for those related services providers, the series of process including the evaluation, Individualized Education Plan, the implementation of Individualized Education Plan and other services provided by them may be questionable for objectiveness and professionalism. On the other hand, a lack of any regulation on this has bad influence for them to do their jobs. It is especially easy to trigger parents' doubts on the qualification on the whole process during those related services providers performing their duties.

---

[55] The Taiwan Special Education Law, Article 23; legislated in 1984, amended in 2013.

Chapter Five
Uncertainty in the Implementation of Special Education in Macau

In the practice of special education in Macau, there are a few procedures that the practitioners should comply themselves with. Most of all, there are four necessary steps before the actual education for special education students begin. These four steps are "identification and referral", "evaluation", "development of Individualized Education Plan and Educational Activities Program" and "placement". These procedures ensure the students with special education needs for having the appropriate education and related services, and for better contribution to their academic study and life. However, some of these contents are not fully covered by the Law No.9/2006, the Decree Law No.33/96/M any other laws related with special education in Macau. There are some defects in the legal system of special education.

The subsequent paragraphs will talk about the procedures that should be concerned while regulating the implementation of special education.

5.1 Identification and referral of students with special education needs

A student should be a "student who has special education needs" under the law, so the student can be eligible to receive special education and the related services. Based on the protection of education right for the students with special education needs, some parties and individuals have to play the role on finding out the specific students who need special education and related services. That is the identification of students with special education needs. Besides, a referral is someone asking the school to determine if the suspected student is a child in need of special education and the related services.

These are the beginning procedures to protect the education right for special education students. In the implementation of the processes, school plays an irreplaceable role.

5.1.1 The present situation about the identification and referral in Macau

In the current situation in Macau, parents, teachers, related personnel or any other appropriate individuals can be the representatives to make the referral to school for further determination of the issue "if the student is a child with special education needs". Parents and teachers are the individuals having the closest relationship with the children. Once they locate the child with some conditions that should be concerned (both in psychology and physiology) during daily life and studying, they can report it to the school and consulting further assistance for a more accurate identification to the student.

Whenever a class is given a math test, a dictation exercise, a jumping practice, a racing or a chapter review, teachers can observe and measure the students' competency of the entire class. The average performance of the entire class can be considered as the competent level, any student doing typically lower than the average may be taken as a determining factor for notice. Once the factor becomes obvious, particularly the factor is not caused by laziness or any other normal factors of the student, the student would be suspected as a student with special education needs. In order to further help the student to have an appropriate education and related services, the teacher should report this situation to the school. Most of the students with special education needs can be identified by this kind of referral. In addition, schools can locate special education students by some group assessments.[1] Like some specialized purpose tests, if some students have very low scores of the test, it may be a base for a referral to the special education process.

In Macau, after the teachers' or parents' referral of the suspected student, school would make the referral to the CPPSSE for further evaluation on whether the student is in need of special education and related services. Normally, school is the one to make referral to the evaluation institute. If the school does not agree that the student is a student with special education needs, the parents can make reservation and move on to the CPPSSE for children's evaluation.

5.1.2 The problems caused by the missing regulation of identification and referral in Macau

There is no regulation about the rights and obligations of identification and referral for students with special education needs in the Law No.9/2006, the Decree Law No.33/96/M or any other laws in Macau. School is the key for the identification and referral for the students with special education needs. We take this situation for granted and forget the potential risk of the missing regulation in the legal system. Actually, if we do not regulate the rights and the obligations for school on identification and referral, it may bring some problems on the implementation of special education.

---

1   Laura Rothstein & Scott F. Johnson Special education law, 4th Ed, (Thousand Oaks, CA: Sage Publications, 2010), pp85-103.

5.1.2.1 Problem one

The schools may have some measurements or group assessments that identify the students with special dedication needs; or the regular classroom teachers may notice something of concern.[2] Schools are *permitted* to do assessments to the students to meet the IDEA obligation to proactively develop policies and procedures for the identification, location, and evaluation of all children with disabilities in the state or local school district.[3]

However, in Macau, there is no relevant law regulates the rights for schools to identify and makes referral for special education students, once the schools take some specialized purpose tests or have group assessments to screen the suspected special education students within the school, parents and students can reject the measurements with any reasons. The schools have no legal basis to continue the process if the screening is questioned or rejected. Furthermore, the parents or students who reject or refuse the screening can take the schools' proactive policies and assessments for identifying the special education students as discriminations. It is understandable that students and parents have concerns about being discriminated after getting a low score in those assessments, and it is probably for those students to be treated differently as "stupid" by others. But they probably have misunderstanding. Receiving special education is a right for those students with special education needs. Instead of discrimination, blindly reject the screening will bring about the loss of chances for proper education.

The law does not give any statement for the permission of schools' right to make their own policy for special education students' identification and

---

2 Laura Rothstein & Scott F. Johnson Special education law, 4th Ed, (Thousand Oaks, CA: Sage Publications, 2010), p86.

3 20 U.S.C section 1412 (a) (3).

referral; it will lead to an exposure for the schools without legal protection, when schools just try to find out who need special education and related services and try to provide the students with a better opportunity to adjust to the society. If students and parents make a lawsuit against school's policy of identification and referral on screening special education students, schools may be put into a very passive position since no articles regulate their right to screen the special education students.

Legislation should prevent this dilemma by regulating the right for schools to proactively develop policies and procedures for identification, location, and evaluation of all children with special education needs. In Article 17 of the Taiwan Special Education Law, the obligation for schools to identify students with special education needs is "nurseries, kindergartens, and all the schools should identify positively or through application for special needs students".[4] This article might be worth learning for the further legislation in Macau. Further more, in the last paragraph of Article 17 of the Taiwan Special Education Law, the provision states that: if the parent/guardian does not give consent to the identification, the authorized institutions should request the parent/guardian or agent to cooperate with them for the benefit of the students.[5] It is clear that once the law gives a statement for school to have the right to identify and to make referral of the special education needs students, the parents will have legal consequence if they object to the school's right to do the assessment for screening the students with special education needs with unreasonable reasons. The education right for students with special education needs is better protected by law in this way. The dispute between schools and parents will be solved. The identification and referral should be written down

---

4   The Taiwan special education law, Article 17; legislated in 1984, amended in 2013.
5   The Taiwan special education law, Article 17; legislated in 1984, amended in 2013.

as part of the procedures for the implementation of special education in law, and the right to have proper education for students with special education needs would not be neglected or interrupted.

5.1.2.2 Problem two

The identification and referral process are parts of the school district's "child find" obligation in the U.S.[6] Schools in the U.S. are required to identify who would be the suspected student with disabilities.[7] The Individuals with Disabilities Education Act in the U.S. stipulates that the identification and referral is an obligation for the school district. The educational system of Macau is different from the U.S., it is a school but it's not the school district playing the main role on finding out the students with special education needs in reality. However, the Individuals with Disabilities Education Act regulates the obligation to a specific one (the school district) in the U.S.[8] This way can avoid a lot of troubles during the implementation of special education and give a better protection to the students' education right.

When the law regulates the obligation of the identification and referral for the students with special education needs to a specific person or institution, the implementation of identification and referral is more operable. We will no longer worry about the negative situation by nonfeasance. Even the nonfeasance may still happen, we can track it down and make it to fulfill its obligation on the legal level. The situation is same in the U.S., if nonfeasance of the identification and referral happen in school, the parents, students or any others can force the school to fulfill its obligation using legal basis (mostly

---

6 34 C.F.R. section 300.111.

7 Laura Rothstein & Scott F. Johnson Special education law, 4th Ed, (Thousand Oaks, CA: Sage Publications, 2010), p85.

8 34 C.F.R. section 300.111.

IDEA and other related laws). The students' concerns of being neglected by school may be greatly reduced in this situation.

Unlike the United States of America, no contents of identification and referral are written down in any laws for the students with special education needs in Macau. It means no one is legally responsible for identification and referral of the special education student. The identification and referral are always implemented by the schools in Macau. Once the schools in Macau are "lazy" on the identification and referral, the students with special education needs would lose his/her opportunity to receive the proper education and related services. This nonfeasance of school would compromise the special education students' future life and damage the purpose of special education.[9] Even worse, due to the fact that no article regulates the obligation for anyone on the identification and referral of the students with special education needs, the neglected students with special education needs and their parents may have no remedy to file their complaints for this situation. This problem is just on the contrary with problem one and put students and parents into a passive position.

The above problems can be easily avoided through legislation in Macau, by filling up the flaw of the missing regulation of identification and referral for students with special education needs. Once the right and obligation of identification and referral are written in the special education law, the nonfeasance will be prevented and the rights of student's education will be better protected.

---

[9] The Decree Law No.33/96/M (the Macau Decree Law of Special Education System), Article 2; the Law Number 9/2006 (the Macau Fundamental Law of Non-Tertiary Education System), Article 12.

5.2 The evaluation of students with special education needs

Nowadays in Macau legal system, Paragraph 2 of Article 12 in the Law No.9/2006 regulates the institution for the evaluation of students with special education need. It says the evaluation will be taken by the public department of the government or the entities authorized by the education department.[10] No other details can be found in the Law No.9/2006 about the evaluation of student with special education needs. However, the Decree Law No.33/96/M regulates "the special conditions of evaluation" in Article 9. It regulates that:[11]

1. *The special conditions of evaluation are defined by the behaviors, the capacity of the student and the nature of curriculum content.*

2. *These contents should be considered as the special conditions of evaluation, namely: a) The type of instrument or the test of evaluation; b) The way of expression; c) The periodicity; d) The duration; e) The location of the test.*

3. *It is up to each teacher, and with the support of other coordination structures and pedagogical supervision, to find the specific and concrete way to evaluate the learning process.*

Article 9 regulates the content of the conditions of evaluation in detail. In the actual operation, once the potential special education student is

---

10 The Law Number 9/2006 (the Macau Fundamental Law of Non-Tertiary Education System), Article 12.

11 The Decree Law No.33/96/M (the Macau Decree Law of Special Education System), Article 9; the article is only in Chinese version or Portuguese version, the above English version is translated by the author.

recommended to the evaluation institute by schools or parents, the evaluation would begin after obtaining the parental consent. The evaluation is the second step for the process of special education's implementation after the identification from the school's referral. Generally speaking, a qualified evaluation for a specific student should answer these questions:

    a. Is the student eligible for the classifications of the Decree Law No.33/96/M or Article 12 of the Law Number 9/2006?

    b. What is the student's academic level?

    c. What kind of special education and related services dose the student need?

The evaluation about whether a student is qualified to receive special education and related services is a series of complicated, professional and systematic work, which, require the coordination of specialists to guarantee equal, scientific, objective, comprehensive and systematic evaluation for the student.[12] To achieve this goal, the law is required for at least regulating "what institutions are qualified to do the evaluation of students with special education needs?", so that we can rely on certain reliable and legal individuals or institutions. The student's education right will not easily be neglected under this circumstance. Moreover, writing those contents in the special education law will reduce unfair evaluation and discrimination to students.

5.2.1 The evaluation institution

We can find that the Paragraph 2 of Article 12 in the Law No.9/2006 says that the students with special education needs shall be designated by the authorized public department or the institution which designated by the

---

12 Hu, Xiaoyi, "Indiscriminative Evaluation in Special Education Law in the United States and Its Implications China", Chinese Journal of Special Education (Monthly), No.2, 2005(Serial No.56).

educational administrative authority.[13] Following this law, at present, the special education schools and the CPPSSE are the institutions for the evaluation of students with special education needs in Macau. Still, the law just points out the evaluation department but no duties and obligations are stated in the provision. However, the departments do a good job through helping the special education needs students.

We can go through some data and principles of the evaluation of students with special education needs from the DSEJ to see how the CPPSSE schools perform their duty in the evaluation.

The goal for the CPPSSE is to evaluate the students with special education needs.[14] It uses professional knowledge to make a scientific plan to increase the student's chances to success in both academic life and social life.[15] In Macau, students with special education needs will be placed in three different kinds of classes in the education system: the inclusive class, the small special education class and the special education class.[16]

The evaluation principle from the CPPSSE and special education schools are based on this general classification to implement their rules to evaluation.

---

13 The Law Number 9/2006 (the Macau Fundamental Law of Non-Tertiary Education System), Paragraph 2 of Article 12.

14 See official statistics of the DSEJ http://portal.dsej.gov.mo/webdsejspace/internet/Inter_main_page.jsp#; accessed on 10th of September, 2014.

15 See official statistics of the DSEJ http://portal.dsej.gov.mo/webdsejspace/internet/Inter_main_page.jsp#; accessed on 10th of September, 2014.

16 See official statistics of the DSEJ http://portal.dsej.gov.mo/webdsejspace/internet/Inter_main_page.jsp#; accessed on 10th of September, 2014.

5.2.1   The Evaluation Principle of Students with Special Education Needs[17]

General classification	Intelligence	Other problems	Education support	Goal
The inclusive student	General	Physical dysfunction	A small amount of special assistance is given for study and school environment	To increase the student's chance to success
		Extensive development disorders (Autism groups obstacles)		
		Attention deficit hyperactivity disorder		
		Specific learning difficulties		
		Long-term and sustained emotional behavioral problems		
	Terminate	Learning difficulty		
	Gifted	Learning or adjustment difficulties		
Small special education class student	General	Long-term and sustained severe emotional behavioral problems	Larger accommodate or assistance is needed	
	Terminate			
	Mild mental retardation	Learning difficulty		
Special education student	Mental retardation	Learning and daily life adjustment difficulties	Individual curriculum and coordination of special education environment	

---

17 See official statistics of the DSEJ http://portal.dsej.gov.mo/webdsejspace/internet/Inter_main_page.jsp#; accessed on 15th of August, 2014; the materials are rearranged and translated by the author.

As we can see, the evaluation principle is very detailed and it tells us what support different kinds of students with special education needs in different classes, and it clearly tells us about how the evaluation is conducted by the CPPSSE and special education schools. Still, how the CPPSSE and the special education schools responsibly evaluate the students with special education needs, help them for the development in study and provide them a better adjusted school environment are simply stayed in practical. The concerned conditions are more specific that Article 9 of the Decree Law No.33/96/M Especially other than the type of instrument or the test of evaluation, the way of expression, the periodicity, the duration and the location of the test,[18] we believe that other conditions in the above form should be stated in legislation as well. All these things are indispensable to the implementation of special education. Whether they should be written in the special education law or other laws remain a necessary topic for further discussion. However, we can at least have one conclusion about the defect of the evaluation provision in the Decree Law No.33/96/M at present: the law of evaluation of special education is falling a lot behind the reality.

On the contrary, we believe that the recent evaluation for students with special education needs will improve the new legislation for the future Macau special education law in a tremendous way.

5.2.2 The composition of the evaluation team

After finding out the answer that "special education school and the CPPSSE which is authorized under the Macau Education and Youth Affairs

---

18 The Decree Law No.33/96/M (the Macau Decree Law of Special Education System), Paragraph 2 of Article 9; the law is only in Chinese version or Portuguese version, the above English version is translated by the author.

Bureau"[19] to the question of "what institutions are responsible to do the evaluation of special education student?",[20] here comes another question: what kind of person is qualified to evaluate the student in those institutions?

Due to the particularity of the special education needs students, and the process of evaluation should be thoroughly enough, the evaluation team should involve with specific specialists to guarantee the scientific and appropriative of the evaluation.

Because the composition of the evaluation team of special education is not mentioned in Article 12 of the Law No.9/2006 and the Decree Law No.33/96/M, the confusion of the composition of the evaluation team would rise. Actually, by regulating who should participate in the evaluation, it can reduce a lot of conflicts about the result of the evaluation. The result would be more reliable and trustworthy with a clear elaboration from legal system instead of a requirement from some related department.

Again, we can see the composition of the evaluation team in reality so that we can tell what the law can be improved in this issue.

The DSEJ requires every special education school (both public and private special education schools) in Macau to build up a professional special education team. This team provides services for evaluating teaching, tutoring and treatment for the students with special education needs, and the CPPSSE will provide the related services to those regular private schools that do not develop professional special education team[21].

There are two kinds of professional special education team in Macau: the

---

19 The Law Number 9/2006 (the Macau Fundamental Law of Non-Tertiary Education System), Article 12.

20 The content in 5.2.1 the evaluation institution of chapter five in this thesis.

21 See official statistics, the Macau Education and Youth Affairs Bureau (DSEJ) http://portal.dsej. gov.mo/webdsejspace/internet/Inter_main_page.jsp#; accessed on 15th of August, 2014

professional special education team of the CPPSSE and the professional special education team of public/private schools. The differences and similarities between the professional special education team of the CPPSSE and the professional special education team of public/private schools are in the following form:

5.2.2 The Composition of the Evaluation Team[22]

Professional special education team	Centre of Psycho-pedagogical Support and Special Education (CPPSSE)	Public/Private schools
The differences and similarities of the composition of professional special education team	Special education teacher	Special education teacher/ Resource teacher
	Psychological counselor	Psychological counselor
	Occupational therapist	Occupational therapist
	Physiotherapist	Physiotherapist
	Language therapist	Language therapist/ Language training teachers
	Student counselor	-

---

22 See official statistics, the Macau Education and Youth Affairs Bureau (DSEJ) http://portal.dsej. gov.mo/webdsejspace/internet/Inter_main_page.jsp#; accessed on 15th of August, 2014; the materials are rearranged and translated by the author.

The compositions in the above professional special education teams are basically the same.[23] The differences are caused by different institutions. However, the functions for these two teams are the same; it means both teams provide the same evaluation to students with special education needs. The evaluation is equal and efficient for each student.

As the purposes of the evaluation are to identify the students with special education needs and to find out what kind of special education and related services the student needs, the specialist of education is required in the evaluation team, and plays a key role on arranging the best special educational plan for the student in a scientific way.

As we know, to identify the students with physical and psychological limitations is not easy, especially the identification of the students with psychological limitations. It requires professional medical knowledge and psychological knowledge; that is why the medical expertise and psychologists should join the evaluation.

On the other hand, the evaluation is pointing to one specific student, so the team should be very familiar with the condition of that student, in that situation, based on the fact that school teachers and student's parents are the people being most familiar with the student's conditions, they should be participate in the evaluation group as well.

The Taiwan Special Education Law is a typical sample on regulating the members of the evaluation team. Taiwan set up the Special Education Students Diagnosis and Placement Counseling Committee (briefly called DPCC), it is a committee for the special education students' evaluation (diagnosis) and placement. Article 6 of the Taiwan Special Education Law states the members

---

23 See official statistics of the DSEJ http://portal.dsej.gov.mo/webdsejspace/internet/Inter_main_ page.jsp#; accessed on 15th of August, 2014; the materials are rearranged and translated by the author.

of the Special Education Students Diagnosis and Placement Counseling Committee in a very detailed way: the DPCC should include scholars and experts, educational and school administrators, delegates of teacher organizations, partners, professionals of special education, and delegates of related institutions and groups.[24] Moreover, the proportion of the members is regulated as well: "Among the members of the aforementioned committee, delegates of educational and school administrators combined are less than a half and those of a single gender less than a third of the total".[25] However, as far as the author concerned, the evaluation of the students with special education needs is a kind of process needing professional medical knowledge, the DPCC may not qualify enough to evaluate the physical or psychological problem of the students. Even more, the number of students that need to be evaluated may be a few dozens, if the composition of the evaluation team is with so many kinds of members, the efficiency may be influenced.[26]

Macau is facing the same problems and even worse, Macau has no law to this issue. Although the DSEJ gives us a comprehensive composition of professional special education team, those teachers and parents that being the most familiar person are excluded from the official statistics.

Of course, the author is not suggesting that laws should be so detailed like Taiwan by regulating all the aspects of evaluation of students with special education needs. The law does not have to be so detailed about this composition of the evaluation team issue. However, a good legislation should be predictable to the future development, and in most of the time, a too tedious legislation can be rigid and dragging the future development. The CPPSSE in

---

24 The Taiwan Special Education Law, Article 6; legislated in 1984, amended in 2013.

25 The Taiwan Special Education Law, Article 6; legislated in 1984, amended in 2013.

26 Hu Yongchong, "The Review of 98-year Edition of Special Education Law", Special Education of Primary School, No.49, June 2010, pp1-9.

Macau can make internal rules instead of listing all of them in Macau special education law. However, making the composition of the evaluation team into the law can not only, prevent the evaluation from the non-qualification of the evaluation members, but also authorize the outcome of the evaluation. Since there is no law regulating the composition of special education student's evaluation team, this still remains as options for the future special education legislation, we can use the content of the composition of evaluation team of students with special education needs in the Taiwan Special Education Law for reference, or leave it to authorized institute or the CPPSSE to decide the details.

5.2.3 Parental consent to the evaluation

In Macau, before the evaluation of special education student begins, the parental consent of the evaluation is required. In the United States of America under IDEA, consent of the evaluation means that "the parent/guardian has been fully informed about all the relevant information of what the school is going to do for the evaluation of the student".[27] Macau has no difference on this aspect. Article 12 in the Law No.9/2006 does not regulate the parental consent of the evaluation. However, the Decree Law No.33/96/M regulates the content of evaluation for students with special education need.

Because of the importance of the parental participation, the law requires that parental attention and agreement occur before an individual evaluation can be made.[28] Like Article 17 of the Taiwan Special Education Law, it states the evaluation can start after obtaining parental consent.[29] We always focus on the students' rights but neglect the parental rights when the issue is related with

---

[27] 34 C.F.R. section 300.9.

[28] Laura Rothstein & Scott F. Johnson, Special education law, 4th Ed, (Thousand Oaks, CA: Sage Publications, 2010), pp87-89.

[29] The Taiwan Special Education Law, Article 17; legislated in 1984, amended in 2013.

special education. The Decree Law No. 33/96/M regulates that the evaluation should obtain the parental consent in Article 16. The article points out that the parental consent should be "expressive consent".[30] It is understandable that parent/guardian may say no when school or other educational agency asks for parental permission for an evaluation for the student. In most cases, if the legal representative (parent/guardian) of the child considers the evaluation may have negative influence on the child and reject the evaluation, since the legal representative (parent/guardian) is the most thoughtful person for the student, the law should take their consent for consideration. That is why Article 16 of the Decree Law No. 33/96/M exists. The law should respect the legal representative's will on the child's evaluation on special education and let the parent have the opportunity to give their opinion to agree or disagree.

However, once the Decree Law No. 33/96/M gives the parental right to refuse the evaluation on a suspected special education need student, the law should regulate that the evaluation institutions and other educators would not take responsibility on the consequence caused by the disagreement from the parent/guardian. Once the evaluation is stopped by the legal representative's disagreement, the student's right for a proper education might be sacrificed.

It is not easy for the law to look for a balance among these factors. It is also essential to understand that the school's obligation is to provide and to ensure proper education for the students, regardless of parents' wishes. While facing the disapproval of evaluation of student from parent/guardian, school or educational agency should take the obligation to inform the parent/guardian. The authorized institute should communicate with the parent/guardian and ask for parental consent. The responsibilities of school and authorized institute

---

30 The Decree Law No. 33/96/M (the Macau Decree Law of Special Education System), Article 16.

should be divided.[31] This may bring a solution to the dilemma above. We should be thoughtful for some situations arise. in, which the parents' thoughts may conflict with the authorized decision. All in all, only by requiring the parents' understanding of their right and informing them of available procedures could the goals of the Decree Law No. 33/96/M be attained.

5.2.4 The validity period of the evaluation

As time goes by, the result of the evaluation for a specific student may be not suitable anymore. The Individualized Education Plan for the student may be useless because the plan of special education and related services was designed based on the evaluation which took place a long time ago. The physiological and psychological conditions of an individual can be easily changed and be influenced by the medical improvement and social environment, and the evaluation of the student may be not suitable any longer. In order to avoid this negative situation, it is essential to make rules on the prescription of the evaluation. The IDEA regulates that the child should be reevaluated at least every three years.[32] Macau has no regulations for the validity period of the evaluation; it may easily cause the situation that one evaluation is a lifelong evaluation. As a matter of fact, it is hard to avoid all the deviation during the evaluation, if reevaluation and the validity period of the evaluation do not be legislated; the student's right for special education is still at risk.[33]

Evaluation is the necessary way to find out what sort of student has

---

31 Guo Meiman, "Analysis of Special Education Law", Special Education of Primary School, 53, June 2012, p13-23.

32 20. U.S.C section 1414(a) (2) (b).

33 Hu Yongchong, "The Review of 98-year Edition of Special Education Law", Special Education of Primary School, No.49, June 2010, pp1-9.

special education need, moreover, it is the important way to identify what kind of special education and related services are appropriate for the student. If the types of special education needs are known and special education programming and related services are implemented, evaluation continue to be necessary to test, so that we can know the special education programming and related services are helpful and effective for the students' special education needs.

These important contents of evaluation are not written in the Decree Law No. 33/96/M or the Law No.9/2006 or any other laws concerning special education. Even they are not well regulated, it does not mean those factors of evaluation of the special education students are not worthy to be written into the related law; it simply means there are legal loopholes for Macau special education law to be filled.

5.3 The Individualized Education Plan and the Educational Activities Program

5.3.1 The generality of the Individualized Education Plan and the Educational Activities Program

After the evaluation of the student and the confirmation of the student are eligible to the legal system, the Individualized Education Plan and the Educational Activities Program must be developed by using the information collected from the evaluation process. To some extent, to develop the Individualized Education Plan and the Educational Activities Program are the most indispensable process for the students with special education needs. Some American scholars said that individualized education plan is the cornerstone of the Individuals with Disabilities Education Act[34] because it is the direction with essential information for school, teacher and other related people to provide a free and appropriate public education (FAPE) from the cases of Honing v. Doe, 1998 and Roland M. v. Concord School Committee, 1990 in the United States of America.[35] To develop the Individualized Education Plan is the core for the implementation of special education[36]. With a similar importance in the U.S.   over the development of the Individualized Education Plan for students with special education needs, it is enlightenment for Macau to figure out the problem of "How to better regulate the Individualized Education Plan and the Educational Activities Program" in legal perspective. The Individualized Education Plan and the Educational Activities Program are not mentioned in the Law No.9/2006. In Macau, the Individualized Education Plan and the Educational Activities Program are the critical components in the Decree Law Number 33/96/M. The provisions state thoroughly about the conditions of a qualified Individualized Education Plan and an Educational Activities Program should include. The Individualized Education Plan and the Educational Activities Program are trying for the best exert of the student's study and potential development.

In Macau, the Individualized Education Plan includes all the necessary information of the student and what special education and related services the student should obtain, in order to improve the academic level. The Educational Activities Program is a plan made around the topic of "how to teach the

---

34 Laura Rothstein & Scott F. Johnson Special education law, 4th Ed, (Thousand Oaks, CA: Sage Publications, 2010), pp117-129.

35 Laura Rothstein & Scott F. Johnson Special education law, 4th Ed, (Thousand Oaks, CA: Sage Publications, 2010), pp117-129.

36 Huang Yongxiu & Zhao Bin, "Policy and Regulation of American Pre-school Special Education and Enlightenment" Chinese Journal of Special Education (Monthly), No.1 (Serial No.97), 2008, pp5-7.

student", for better implement the Individualized Education Plan. Relevant measure and academic goal of the student are included in the Educational Activities Program. They complete each other in the implementation of special education, and they are legally tied to each other.

The Individualized Education Plan and the Educational Activities Program should be renewed at the beginning of each academic year and can be reformulated by the governing body of the authorized educational institution.[37] That means the teacher who plays the main role on implementing special education at school to students with special education needs is not the one who has the legal right to do the adjustment for the Individualized Education Plan and the Educational Activities Program. The other paragraph about the renovation and redesign of the plan and program of Article 15 of the Decree Law Number 33/96/M regulates that the evaluation of the Individualized Education Plan and the Educational Activities Program are carried out by all teachers and specialized technicians involved, and are approved by the governing body of the authorized educational institution.[38] The Individualized Education Plan and Educational Activities Program are made by the professional team of special education which we talked about it in the part of "The teachers under the related special education law in Macau"[39] and "The Related Service Providers under the related special education law in Macau"[40]. Those team members are the persons using their professional knowledge to develop the Individualized Education Plan for the students with special

---

[37] The Decree Law No.33/96/M (the Macau Decree Law of Special Education System), Paragraph 1 of Article 15.

[38] The Decree Law No.33/96/M (the Macau Decree Law of Special Education System), Paragraph 2 of Article 15.

[39] See the previous content of Chapter Four.

[40] See the previous content of Chapter Four.

education needs. Other than these members, the development should include the parental consent.[41] Developing an appropriate, scientific and operable Individualized Education Plan and Educational Activities Program are the key processes to ensure the future development of the students with special education needs. Sometimes the student can participate in the development of his/her Individualized Education Plan if the circumstance is suitable.

5.3.2 The Individualized Education Plan

5.3.2.1 The content of the Individualized Education Plan in the Decree Law of 33/96/M

There are a few things to be considered during the development of the Individualized Education Plan and the Educational Activities Program for the students with special education needs, such as the result of the evaluation, the advantages and disadvantages of the student, the potential and talent, the academic level and what is good for the future development of the student and so on. Otherwise, it has to address developmental and functional needs that can include a variety of matters beyond academics.[42]

Under the Decree Law No.33/96/M, the Individualized Education Plan is supposed to be a package for the application of the special education system rising to the preparation, this package includes the following content[43]:

a. Identification of the student.

---

[41] The Decree Law No.33/96/M (the Macau Decree Law of Special Education System), h) of Article 12.

[42] Laura Rothstein & Scott F. Johnson Special education law, 4th Ed, (Thousand Oaks, CA: Sage Publications, 2010), pp117-129.

[43] The Decree Law No.33/96/M (the Macau Decree Law of Special Education System), Article 12.

b. Summary of school history and other relevant background, namely the degree of effectiveness of the measures previously adopted.

c. Characteristics of the student about the potential, level of knowledge acquisitions and problem of knowledge acquisitions.

d. Medical diagnosis and the necessary recommendations of educational health services.

e. The evaluation of participation level when student joined the institution's activity.

f. The special education measures that to be applied.

g. Date of the plan making and signature of the participants.

h. Acknowledgement of the guardian.

i. General guidance on the areas and appropriate special curricula for the student.

j. The identification of support department that provides services to students.

Ten points are included in this article. Considering all perspectives will be related to the necessary information about the development of the student, we can see that legislation of the Decree Law No.33/96/M pays lots of attention to the Individualized Education Plan for the students with special education needs.

All the students identified as students with special education needs (including those students with special education needs in inclusive class, in small special education class and in special education class) must have their own Individualized Education Plan.[44]

---

44 See official statistics of the DSEJ http://portal.dsej.gov.mo/webdsejspace/internet/Inter_main_ page.jsp#; accessed on 15th of August, 2014.

5.3.2.2 The confusion in the article of the Individualized Education Plan

Parents are playing an irreplaceable role during the development of the Individualized Education Plan for his/her child. The level of the parental participation can strongly influence the result of the implementation of the Individualized Education Plan.

However, as far as the author concerned, the provision about the protection of the parental right of the development of the Individualized Education Plan is not enough.

In the Decree Law No.33/96/M, two places concerning the parental right are mentioned separately in Article 12: the Individualized Education Plan and Article 16: the consent of parents or guardian. Both articles talk about that the parent has the right to acknowledge the development of the Individualized Education Plan of his/her child. As we discussed above, the parental right of evaluation of the students with special education needs is that "the evaluation should be consented by the parent/guardian".[45] Consent means that the parent is fully informed about all the details related to what the evaluation would be involved and what kind of influence would bring to the child.[46] However, the parental right for the development of the Individualized Education Plan is acknowledgement instead of consent in the law. The related institute has to provide the Individualized Education Plan to the parent/guardian after the development process finishes. However, only an acknowledgement of this important issue of the child is far away from enough. This regulation means

45 The Decree Law No.33/96/M (the Macau Decree Law of Special Education System), Article 16.

46 Laura Rothstein & Scott F. Johnson Special education law, 4th Ed, (Thousand Oaks, CA: Sage Publications, 2010).

the parent/guardian can be excluded from the whole process during the development of the Individualized Education Plan of the child, and simply just be informed of the outcome. Actually, parent/guardian should participate in the process of development of the Individualized Education Plan instead of acknowledgement.[47] The law of special education shall at least regulate the parental consent in this issue like the consent right of evaluation of their child written in the Decree Law No.33/96/M instead of "Acknowledgement of the guardian[48]".

The Individualized Education Plan is a document that includes a variety of information about the student with special education needs. A scientific, proper and operable Individualized Education Plan is the key to help the students with special education needs for future development. Even the Decree Law No.33/96/M regulates the content of the Individualized Education Plan very thoughtfully, it does not fully recognize the importance of the parental participation and such regardlessness has become one of the defects in the special educational legal system.

5.3.3 The content of the Educational Activities Program in the Decree Law No.33/96/M

If we say that the Individualized Education Plan is a plan for understanding "what are the special elements of the student", and then the Educational Activities Program is a plan for "How to teach the student with special education needs".

Under the Decree Law No.33/96/M, the Educational Activities Program

---

47 The Decree Law No.33/96/M (the Macau Decree Law of Special Education System), Article 12 and Article 16.

48 The Decree Law No.33/96/M (the Macau Decree Law of Special Education System), Paragraph 1 of Article 12.

is a package for the application of the special education system rising to the preparation, this package includes:[49]

> a). *the level of capability or competence of the student in curriculum content areas or specified curriculum in the Individualized Education Plan;*
>
> b). *the objectives to be achieved;*
>
> c). *the methodological guidelines to be adopted;*
>
> d). *the system, process and criteria for their evaluation of the student;*
>
> e). *to distribute the tasks of program to the responsible technicians in school;*
>
> f). *the time distribution of provided educational activities;*
>
> g). *the schedule of the various educational activities;*
>
> h). *the evaluation of the methodologies and results for the Educational Activities Program;*
>
> i). *the signing of the technicians who took part in the elaboration.*

As far as the author is concerned, some of the other content in the Decree Law No.33/96/M should be included in the Educational Activities Program. Article 9 is the regulation about the special conditions for student's assessment. Some of the contents within the clause can be included in the scope of the Educational Activities Program. They have many similarities. From the very beginning, the special assessment conditions are defined as taking the behavior, capabilities of the student and the nature of the curriculum content which

---

[49] The Decree Law No.33/96/M (the Macau Decree Law of Special Education System), a) – i) of Paragraph 1, Article 13; the law is only in Chinese version or Portuguese version, the above English version is translated by the author.

conform to the request of "consider the capability or competence of the student in curriculum content areas or specified curriculum in the Individualized Education Plan".[50] Secondly, the contents themselves of special assessment conditions are parts of what the Educational Activities Program should consider. The contents of special assessment conditions includes: the type of assessment or exam; the way or means of expression; the periodicity; the duration; the location of the exam.[51] All these contents should be considered during the development of the Educational Activities Program. In the legal perspective, it is not necessary to redo it separately if the scopes are nearly the same. Why not just put those similar contents of special assessment conditions into the article of the development of the Individualized Education Plan? Or combine the Individualized Education Plan and the Educational Activities Program together? This is a win-win situation; one is to reduce the teacher's workload by doubling efforts in the similar area, the other is to increase the effectiveness of the implementation of Macau special education law.

5.4 Placement

After the evaluation, once the student is eligible as a student with special education needs according to the legal system, the matter of placement comes. Due to Paragraph 3 of Article 12 of the Law No.9/2006 states that special education preferentially develops inclusive education in regular school, may also take place in the institutions of special education through other forms;[52]

---

50 The Decree Law No.33/96/M (the Macau Decree Law of Special Education System), Article 13.

51 The Decree Law No.33/96/M (the Macau Decree Law of Special Education System), Article 9.

52 The Law Number 9/2006 (the Macau Fundamental Law of Non-Tertiary Education System), Paragraph 3 of Article 12.

and inclusive education becomes the primary option for the placement of students with special education needs in Macau.

Nowadays in Macau, the CPPSSE divide the students with special education needs into three kinds and put them in different classes for further special education in educational system:[53]

    a. The inclusive student in regular class.

    b. The student with study ability worse than regular student.

    c. The student with retarded and multiple disorders.

These three kinds of students are classified because different classes are providing different kinds of special education and related services based on the characteristics of the student's physiological and psychological situation. Based on the characteristics of each kind, the learning focuses and teaching methods are redesigned. The characteristics of the student's physiological and psychological situation will be evaluated by the school's professional team of special education or the professional team of the CPPSSE in Macau.[54] The placement of these three kinds of classes are very well implemented in Macau, but no provisions of the Law No.9/2006 or the Decree Law No.33/96/M mention any details of them, which makes the legal system obsolete and derive the classes of legal basis.

---

53 See official statistics of the DSEJ http://portal.dsej.gov.mo/webdsejspace/internet/Inter_main_page.jsp#; accessed on 1st October, 2014.

54 See official statistics of the DSEJ http://portal.dsej.gov.mo/webdsejspace/internet/Inter_main_page.jsp#; accessed on 1st October, 2014.

5.2.1   Three Kinds of Special Education Classes in Macau[55]

Classification	Student number	School Distribution
Inclusive class	Number of total student per class: 25 Number of inclusive student: 3	Public and private school: kindergarten, primary school and middle school
Small class of special education	Number of total student per class: 8-15	Public school: primary school and middle school (special education course of vocational and technical)
Special education class	Number of total student per class: 6-15	Public school: three levels divided by mild, moderate and severe Private school: primary school and middle school (divided by mild, moderate and severe) / No clear stages

Actually, the amount of students with special education needs is not a small number. They are all counting on the legal protection to ensure their educational right. More than 1,300 students received special education and related services in the 2013/2014 academic year (see the related data in the form of "the Details of Students with Special Education Needs").[56] Evidently, the number of inclusive students in private school was increasing rapidly in the past few years. We can tell that this situation is caused by the implementation

---

55 See official statistics of the DSEJ http://portal.dsej.gov.mo/webdsejspace/internet/Inter_main_page.jsp#; official statistics of the DSEC http://www.dsec.gov.mo/default.aspx?noredirect=true; both accessed in 20th of June, 2014.

56 See official statistics of the DSEJ http://www.dsej.gov.mo/cappee/cappee08/se/se5.html; accessed on 10th of September, 2014.

of the Law No.9/2006 about the content of "special education preferentially develops inclusive education in regular school, can also take place in the institutions of special education through other forms" in Paragraph 3 of Article 12.[57]

At present, the limitation for having an inclusive class is that the inclusive students cannot be more than three persons; the total number of an inclusive class cannot be more than 25.[58] The number of different kinds of placements for school to receive students with special education needs may help us to see the implementation situation of Article 12 of the Law No.9/2006.

5.4   The Placement Number of Schools Receiving Students with Special Education Needs[59]

Placement / School Type	Inclusive Class	Small Class of Special Education	Special Education Class
Public School	9	2	5
Private School	28	-	4
Total number	37	2	9

The above form shows us that the implementation of "special education preferentially develops inclusive education in regular school, special education may also take place in the institutions of special education through other

---

57 The Law Number 9/2006 (the Macau Fundamental Law of Non-Tertiary Education System), Paragraph 3 of Article 12.

58 See official statistics of the DSEJ http://portal.dsej.gov.mo/webdsejspace/internet/Inter_main_ page.jsp#; accessed on 17th of August, 2014.

59 See official statistics of the DSEJ http://portal.dsej.gov.mo/webdsejspace/internet/Inter_main_ page.jsp#; accessed on 17th of August, 2014.

forms"[60] is pleased by the observation of the data. The level of inclusive education in Macau has not achieved full inclusive education, and most of the people are holding the negative attitude towards full inclusive education thinking it may not be the best way to students with special education needs, and it may be hard for all the non special educational teachers to provide appropriate education to those students with special education needs[61]. So, other than inclusive education in regular class, special education can be applied in other forms like small special education class in regular school and special education class in special education school. We can tell the way that leaving other kinds of special education available is the law admitting that sometimes or to some specific students with special education needs, the separation of education with other regular students may be necessary and suitable for them to have a more appropriate education and may not cause undue disruption to other students.[62]

Actually, with no other regulations to support Paragraph 3 of Article 12 of the Law No.9/2006 about the content of preferentially development of inclusive education in regular school, it is not always smooth to implement this legal requirement in Macau.

5.4.1 The rejection of the placement by regular schools

We know that the CPPSSE is playing the role to help the evaluated

---

60 The Law Number 9/2006 (the Macau Fundamental Law of Non-Tertiary Education System), Paragraph 3 of Article 12.

61 Katie Shultz Stout, "Special Education Inclusion" http://weac.org/the Articles/specialedinc/; accessed on 17th of September, 2014.

62 Laura Rothstein & Scott F. Johnson Special education law, 4th Ed, (Thousand Oaks, CA: Sage Publications, 2010), pp171-198.

special education students to look for educational placement from schools, and it depends on the student's evaluated situation for decision of placement in a regular school or in a special education school.

When inclusive education becomes a primary option for the CPPSSE to consider, and no other operable legal support is helping the implementation, there is a dilemma for the CPPSSE to put the placement into force. The conflict of the disagreement about the placement of student with special education needs is the most intense topic; it brings litigation in Macau special education. Students with special education needs and their parents have to accept that no legal support is standing in this situation.

When the disagreement of placement of students with special education needs happens, first of all, we should know why special education in Macau preferentially develops inclusive education in regular school rather than other kinds of special education. The concepts of inclusive education has broadly disseminated since the United Nations Educational, Scientific, and Cultural Organization (UNESCO) defined inclusive education as "a process of strengthening the capacity of an education system to reach out to all learners".[63] The worldwide inclusive education for children and youth with disabilities movement lasted for more than four decades and the beginning were the passages of the Individuals with Disabilities Education Act.[64] The philosophy of inclusive education is mostly under the following principles:

One is that putting special education student in a separated educational circumstance with regular students may easily cause the self-fulfilling

---

63 The United Nations Educational, Scientific, and Cultural Organization, 2008a, p9.

64 Kim Fong Poon-McBrayer & Ping-man Wong "Inclusive education services for children and youth with disabilities: Values, roles and challenges of school leaders", Children and Youth Services Review, 35 (2013) pp1520-1525, http://www.journals.elsevier.com/children-and-youth-services-review; accessed on 17th of September, 2014.

prophecy problem of the students with special education needs[65]. This problem will cross out the variety of the student, leading the student in some "particular forms" and potentially be an antidevelopment of the student's talent. The other principle is that inclusive education will bring advantages to both students with disabilities and without disabilities by the interaction to each other.[66]

5.4.2 The perception of the core value of inclusive education in regular schools with inclusion classes

When we acknowledge the benefits of inclusive education, and realize that it can better protect the students' future development and education right, then it is not hard for us to understand why inclusive education is extensively reformed and practiced through the world. However, this only stands on the perspective on the student's benefits. When we stand on the perspective of the regular school, the dilemma will happen. In Macau, there were cases that the private schools refuse to accept the placement of the students with special education needs from the arrangement of the CPPSSE. The subsequent form may give us a more direct picture about the feeling of inclusive education within the people related with Macau special education. This form is an outcome of the research questionnaire about the schools applying inclusive education in Macau:

---

[65] Laura Rothstein & Scott F. Johnson "Special Education Law," 4th edition, SAGE Publication, Inc. 2010, p171-198.

[66] Laura Rothstein & Scott F. Johnson "Special Education Law," 4th edition, SAGE Publication, Inc. 2010, pp171-198. The chapter of Placement and Leased Restrictive Environment in the book talks about the relationship with special education placement and Leased Restrictive Environment. Through the chapter, the principles of inclusive education are similar with the meaning of Leased Restrictive Environment principles. In this Article, these two contents will be discussed into two topics.

5.4.2   The Perception of the Core Value of Inclusive Education in Regular Schools with Inclusion Classes [67]

School principal	Strongly Disagree	Disagree	Agree	Strongly Agree	Valid Sample
A1.1 Inclusive Education can provide equal study appointee for students with special education needs	0%	18.5%	63%	18.5%	27
A1.2 It is a fundamental right for students with special education needs receiving education in regular classroom	0%	0%	81.5%	18.5%	27
A1.3 Inclusive Education represents the social justice and fairness	0%	0%	81.5%	18.5%	27
A1.4 Inclusive Education is a symbol of civilization	0%	0%	77.8%	22.2%	27
A1.5 It is a discrimination to exclude the students with special education needs out of regular classroom	0%	26.9%	53.8%	19.2%	26

[67] The Centre for Special Education needs and Inclusive Education of The Hong Kong Institute of Education, "The Customized Research of Special Education in Macau". This researcher is authorized by the DSEJ. The research team did the questionnaire and case study during April to July, 2011 and collected quantities of statistics related with special education of Macau and did the forward analysis. And the form of "The perception of the core value of inclusive education in Macau in regular schools with inclusion classes" is the contents in Appendix Four of this report.

Teacher	Strongly Disagree	Disagree	Agree	Strongly Agree	Valid Sample
A1.1 Inclusive Education can provide equal study appointee for students with special education needs	0%	10.1%	80.4%	9.4%	138
A1.2 It is a fundamental right for students with special education needs receiving education in regular classroom	0.7%	5.1%	86.1%	8%	173
A1.3 Inclusive Education represents the social justice and fairness	0%	12.2%	77.7%	10.1%	139
A1.4 Inclusive Education is a symbol of civilization	0%	14.2%	75.2%	10.6%	141
A1.5 It is a discrimination to exclude the students with special education needs out of regular classroom	0.7%	33.8%	54.7%	10.8%	139
Therapist and assistant	Strongly Disagree	Disagree	Agree	Strongly Agree	Valid Sample
A1.1 Inclusive Education can provide equal study appointee for students with special education needs	2.2%	15.6%	62.2%	20%	45
A1.2 It is a fundamental right for students with special education needs receiving education in regular classroom	0%	6.7%	66.7%	26.7%	45

A1.3 Inclusive Education represents the social justice and fairness	0%	11.4%	75%	13.6%	44
A1.4 Inclusive Education is a symbol of civilization	0%	4.4%	68.9%	26.7%	45
A1.5 It is a discrimination to exclude the students with special education needs out of regular classroom	0%	15.9%	61.4%	22.7%	44
Teaching assistant	Strongly Disagree	Disagree	Agree	Strongly Agree	Valid Sample
A1.1 Inclusive Education can provide equal study appointee for students with special education needs	0%	5.9%	76.5%	17.6%	17
A1.2 It is a fundamental right for students with special education needs receiving education in regular classroom	0%	5.9%	70.6%	23.6%	17
A1.3 Inclusive Education represents the social justice and fairness	0%	5.9%	82.4%	11.8%	17
A1.4 Inclusive Education is a symbol of civilization	0%	0%	75%	25%	16
A1.5 It is a discrimination to exclude the students with special education needs out of regular classroom	6.2%	37.5%	43.7%	12.5%	16

Parent	Strongly Disagree	Disagree	Agree	Strongly Agree	Valid Sample
A1.1 Inclusive Education can provide equal study appointee for students with special education needs	0%	1.9%	68.9%	29.1%	103
A1.2 It is a fundamental right for students with special education needs receiving education in regular classroom	0%	3.8%	68.6%	27.6%	105
A1.3 Inclusive Education represents the social justice and fairness	1%	1%	76.5%	21.6%	102
A1.4 Inclusive Education is a symbol of civilization	0%	6.9%	65.3%	27.7%	101
A1.5 It is a discrimination to exclude the students with special education needs out of regular classroom	1%	15%	51%	33%	100

From the percentages of strongly disagreement and disagreement of question A1.1 to A.1.5 in the above form, we can tell there are a few negative perception of inclusive education among the related special education individuals in the schools with inclusion classes, not to mention those regular schools without inclusion classes. As far as the author is concerned, these may be the reasons why some schools refuse to receive the students with special education needs. There are three main reasons causing the negative perception: a. the philosophy of inclusive education concept is not fully embraced by those individuals; b. the school is against the extra pressure brought by the students with special education needs base on: once the school accept it, there will be lots of extra work for school and teachers to implement; c. the parents of regular students give pressure to the school to not to accept special education students.

Of course, prejudice and misunderstanding will always exist in the society, but if those negative and one-sided opinions bring too much obstruction, then the right of students with special education needs may endanger. Thus, laws for stopping the intervention to avoid this situation from continuing in Macau are needed.

5.4.3 Summary

Like Article 22 of the Taiwan Special Education Law says that "all the schools and test centers must not reject student admission to school or test for the sake of disability itself"[68]. We leave the possibly legal loophole about "schools and test centers can reject student admission to school or test for the sake of other element instead of disability itself"[69] aside; this article is a legal solution for regular schools' rejection of application of the inclusive education students. Even more, this article of the Taiwan Special Education Law conforms to the principle of "Zero Reject". The principal concept for the Zero Reject is one of the basic principles from the Amendment of The Individuals with Disabilities Education Act in 1997 in the U.S. Zero Reject becomes a worldwide concept while facing the problem of special education. Legislation of Macau can use this principle to better regulate the situation when the rejection of inclusive education students in regular schools happens.

However, the law of inclusive education just stopped on the statutory of

---

68 The Taiwan Special Education Law, Article 22; legislated in 1984, amended in 2013.

69 Hu Yongchong, "The Review of 98-year Edition of Special Education Law", Special Education of Primary School, No.49, June 2010, pp1-9.

Paragraph 3 of Article 12 of the Law No.9/2006. No other operative articles can support this law in the legal system, it allows the school to say no to the placement of students with special education needs without "justice reason" but without legal consequences. It puts the education right of the student in danger. Otherwise, with a legal support related with Zero Reject, the implementation of Paragraph 3 of Article 12 of the Law No.9/2006 will be more comprehensive than the recent situation while preferentially developing the inclusive education in regular school in Macau.

5.5　The cost issue

About the cost issue, the Law No.9/2006 regulates that one of the methods for government to create conditions to promote development of special education is to provide financial support to the entities which provide special education.[70] But it is not a very operable article with so little detail. As we all know, implementing special education and related services require large amount of efforts and money. Not all the families having children with special education needs can fully cover all the expenses to support their children to have an appropriate education. In order to protect the education right to every child and to ensure those students with special education needs to a proper education, the government is responsible to support them to achieve the goal of the legislation of special education. Financing is one of the most essential support that the government can and should provide. In addiction, the legislative council passed a few laws and regulations to ensure the legitimacy of responsibility of the government on the perspective of funding the special education and related services.

---

[70] The Law Number 9/2006 (the Macau Fundamental Law of Non-Tertiary Education System), Article 12.

If we start to talk about the regulation of the cost issue of special education, we first should have a concept about the education funding in Macau. Macau government provides a good amount of monetary support on education, from the beginning in 1991. The educational financial budget accounted for a significant proportion that was up to 10% of the total fiscal revenue.[71] The proportion maintained in a stable way in a few years. From the very beginning of the implementation of inclusive education in the same year in 1991, Macau government allocated funds for improvement to further develop and better help those students with special education needs. Not until 1995, the implementation of free education by Macau government brought the education system into a new level. In 1997, the proportion of educational financial budget had a bigger improvement and increased to 12% in the total fiscal revenue.[72] It is true that the increasing financial funding is helpful for the improvement of special education, but it is not equal to the quality improvement of special education.[73] However, putting the quality of the teachers and related services providers of special education aside, it is good to see the government pays more attention to it by providing more financial support. On 2002/2003 academic year, the free allowance of special education reached over 8,000,000 MOP.[74] Until 2004/2005 academic year, the free allowance of special education has reached over 9,000,000 MOP per year.[75]

---

[71] Wang Sisi & Lei Jianghua "The inclusive education and enlightenment" (澳門的融合教育及啟示), A JOURNAL OF MODERN SPECIAL EDUCATION, May 2009, pp40-41.

[72] Wang Sisi & Lei Jianghua "The inclusive education and enlightenment" (澳門的融合教育及啟示), A JOURNAL OF MODERN SPECIAL EDUCATION, May 2009, pp40-41.

[73] Hu Yongchong, "The Review of 98-year Edition of Special Education Law", Special Education of Primary School, No.49, June 2010, pp1-9.

[74] Wang Sisi & Lei Jianghua "The inclusive education and enlightenment" (澳門的融合教育及啟示), A JOURNAL OF MODERN SPECIAL EDUCATION, May 2009, pp40-41.

[75] Wang Sisi & Lei Jianghua "The inclusive education and enlightenment" (澳門的融合教育及啟示), A JOURNAL OF MODERN SPECIAL EDUCATION, May 2009, pp40-41.

Further more, on 2005/2006 academic year, on funding the development of special education, except the original funding, the government also provided monetary support for schools and educational institute to add possessions on special educational related facilities and treatment tools and for teacher trainings.[76]

At present, public schools imply free education. The private schools that signed agreement with the government no longer charge fees from the students; however, these expenses are covered by government funding instead of students' families.

The Law No.9/2006 regulates that one of the methods for government to create conditions to promote development of special education is to provide financial support to the entities which provide special education.[77] The DSEJ provides related services to students with special education needs. In compliance with this law, it mandates the eligible schools to receive funding from the fiscal revenue of Macau government. With the financial funding increasing stably in the coming academic years, Article 4, Article 5 and Article 10 of the Decree Law No.33/96/M can be better implemented in practice. These articles are mainly built up on financial basis, with the economic support ensured by Article 12 of the Law No.9/2006, those articles will be easier and better to be implemented.

5.5.1 The contents of free education allowance for special education

Due to Paragraph 5 of Article 12 of the Law No.9/2006 saying that the

---

[76] See official statistics of the DSEJ http://portal.dsej.gov.mo/webdsejspace/internet/Inter_main_page.jsp#; accessed on 15th of August, 2014.

[77] The Law Number 9/2006 (the Macau Fundamental Law of Non-Tertiary Education System), Article 12.

government should support the special education providing institutes on financial backups,[78] the free education allowance for special education covers a variety of fees during the educational process in those institutes. At present, based on the different types of the implementation of special education in Macau, the financial budgets are allotted in different ways. The ways are divided into the funding for each special education class and for each inclusive student.

5.5.1.1   The financial funding for special education classes

For the special education classes that funded by the government authorized department, the DSEJ mainly provides the following few kinds of financial supports to them. Those financial supports for special education classes are:[79]

> a. The special education operational funding;
>
> b. The extra allowance for homogeneous grouping arrangement;
>
> c. The fixed subsidy for supporting the professional special education team;
>
> d. The funding for the program of school development.

Each kind of financial support has its own detailed regulations made by the government for implementing the special education scientifically and efficiently.

---

[78] The Law Number 9/2006 (the Macau Fundamental Law of Non-Tertiary Education System), Article 12.

[79] See official statistics of the DSEJ http://portal.dsej.gov.mo/webdsejspace/internet/Inter_main_page.jsp#; accessed on 15th of August, 2014.

5.5.1.1.1 The special education classes operational funding

The special education classes operational funding is the main part of the monetary support for the special education classes from the DSEJ. This funding aims for maintaining the smooth operation of the class.

5.5.1.1.1 The Special Education Operational Funding of Each Education Stages of Special Education Class in Recent Academic Years[80]

Academic Year / Education Stage	2011/2012 Academic Years	2012/2013 Academic Years	2013/2014 Academic Years
Preschool	570,000 MOP	605,000 MOP	755,000 MOP
Primary school	600,000 MOP	640,000 MOP	807,000 MOP
Middle school	770,000 MOP	820,000 MOP	1,008,000 MOP
High School	870,000 MOP	930,000 MOP	1,143,000 MOP
Special Education Class without Education Stage Division	600,000 MOP	640,000 MOP	807,000 MOP

The above data is arranged from the database of the official website of the DSEJ. Normally, each special education class has 8 to 15 special education students. The data we can see are for each special education class in one academic year. Furthermore, in the current Macau educational system, each regular class have 24 to 45 students, the financial assistance from the DSEJ for special education class equals to each regular class in the same education stage.

---

[80] See official statistics of the DSEJ http://www.dsej.gov.mo/cappee/cappee08/se/se5.html; accessed on 15th of August, 2014; the materials are rearranged and translated by the author.

That means 8 to 15 students with special education needs in one class can use the budget as much as 24 to 45 regular students in a class. Paragraph 5 of Article 12 of the Law No.9/2006 is well implemented by providing sufficient financial support in this way. In one perspective it tells us that implying special education needs a big financial budget, in the other perspective it tells us the government provides a great deal of financial support to develop a better and more efficient circumstance for students in special education classes so that the aims for special education can be ensured. On the other hand, not only the government fulfills its responsibility of "Providing financial support to organizations that teach special education",[81] but also the Decree Law No. 33/96/M can be better implemented in some certain ways.

5.5.1.1.2 The extra allowance for homogeneous grouping arrangement

The policy of funding extra educational allowance to the homogeneous grouping arrangement was started in the academic year of 2011/2012 to encourage the private special education school to arrange those students with similar needs of special education into the same class. To prevent from the uneven intermingled situation, there are two levels for the homogeneous grouping arrangement, the mild level and the severe level. Different levels have different amount of funding when the class reaches some extent of student number.

Normally, if the student number reaches to 11 to 15, the extra allowance will be provided a certain amount of financial support to each class by the DSEJ.

---

[81] The Law Number 9/2006 (the Macau Fundamental Law of Non-Tertiary Education System), Paragraph 5 of Article 12.

5.5.1.1.2   The Extra Allowance for Homogeneous Grouping Arrangement (Mild Level)[82]

Education Stage / Academic Year	Preschool	Primary school	Middle school	High School
2011/2012 Academic Year	213,750 MOP	225,000 MOP	288,750 MOP	326,250 MOP
2012/2013 Academic Year	226,875 MOP	240,000 MOP	307,500 MOP	348,750 MOP
2013/2014 Academic Year	283,125 MOP	302,625 MOP	378,000 MOP	428,625 MOP

5.5.1.1.2   The Extra Allowance for Homogeneous Grouping Arrangement (Severe Level)[83]

Education Stage	Student Number	2011/2012 Academic Year	2012/2013 Academic Year	2013/2014 Academic Year
Preschool	6	142,500 MOP	151,250 MOP	188,750 MOP
Preschool	7	166,250 MOP	176,458 MOP	220,208 MOP
Preschool	8	190,000 MOP	201,667 MOP	251,667 MOP
Primary school	6	150,000 MOP	160,000 MOP	201,750 MOP
Primary school	7	175,000 MOP	186,667 MOP	235,375 MOP
Primary school	8	200,000 MOP	213,333 MOP	269,000 MOP

---

[82] See official statistics of the DSEJ http://www.dsej.gov.mo/cappee/cappee08/se/se5.html; accessed on 15th of August, 2014; the materials are rearranged and translated by the author.

[83] See official statistics of the DSEJ http://www.dsej.gov.mo/cappee/cappee08/se/se5.html; accessed on 15th of August, 2014; the materials are rearranged and translated by the author.

Education Stage	Student Number	2011/2012 Academic Year	2012/2013 Academic Year	2013/2014 Academic Year
Middle school	6	192,500 MOP	205,000 MOP	252,000 MOP
	7	224,583 MOP	239,167 MOP	294,000 MOP
	8	256,667 MOP	273,333 MOP	336,000 MOP
High School	6	217,500 MOP	232,500 MOP	285,750 MOP
	7	253,750 MOP	271,250 MOP	333,375 MOP
	8	290,000 MOP	310,000 MOP	381,000 MOP

The data is given by the official website of the DSEJ, as we can see, the regulations for mild level and severe level are very different and the amount of financial support are not the same at all. The DSEJ stipulates policies which are suitable for the practice situation while implementing special education in Macau. The severe level students need more help and certainly, the severe level classes should be grouped with fewer students so that the special education teacher can be more efficient to help and teach them, and the monetary support ought to be more than the mild classes based on the situation that they need extra equipment or extra helper to better implement special education.

5.5.1.1.3 The fixed subsidy for professional special education team

Except from the special education classes operational funding and the extra allowance for homogeneous grouping arrangement, the fixed subsidy for professional special education team is the third way of financial support for government to provide to private special education schools while implementing special education.

5.5.1.1.3   The Fixed Subsidy for Professional Special Education Team[84]

Academic Year	2011/2012	2012/2013	2013/2014
person / year	244,000 MOP	305,280 MOP	328,790 MOP

As we discussed in Chapter Three of the Special Education Related Service Providers, we know that during the implementation of special education, the CPPSSE organizes those special education and related services providers to group into a professional team, and use the team to help the students with special education needs. The major salaries of the related services providers and fees coming form the related services are covered by the Macau government. Besides, the form "the Fixed Subsidy for Professional Special Education Team" shows that the government is fulfilling its obligation of "Providing financial support to organizations that teach special education"[85] and "Supporting organizations that promote services related to special education"[86] by paying the fixed subsidy for professional special education team. We know the professional special education team is very valuable in the whole process of implementation of special education. As a good result, we are glad to see that the government is taking the obligation of special education part of the Law No.9/2006 and funding the professional special education team.

---

[84] See official statistics of the DSEJ http://www.dsej.gov.mo/cappee/cappee08/se/se5.html; accessed on 15th of August, 2014; the materials are rearranged and translated by the author.

[85] The Law Number 9/2006 (the Macau Fundamental Law of Non-Tertiary Education System), Paragraph 5 of Article 12.

[86] The Law Number 9/2006 (the Macau Fundamental Law of Non-Tertiary Education System), Paragraph 5 of Article 12.

5.5.1.1.4 The funding for the program of school development

This program is to assist schools in improving the environment of schools, adding special educational equipments, teaching tools and conducting related activities for the students with special education needs. In the Decree Law No. 33/96/M, Article 4[87] and Article 5[88] require that the schools should have barrier-free environment and the equipment for special education should be qualified enough. The funding for the program of school development is exactly provided by the government to support the schools to fulfill the articles in the Decree Law No.33/96/M. Even this funding is not fixed, the amount of it is supposed to be adequate.

5.5.1.2 The financial funding for inclusive students

Other than the special education funding for special education classes, the government also support the inclusive students in the educational system.

---

[87] The Decree Law No. 33/96/M (the Macau Decree Law of Special Education System), Article 4 is "Special Equipment".

[88] The Decree Law No. 33/96/M (the Macau Decree Law of Special Education System), Article 4 is "Adaptations of the School Physical Environment".

5.5.1.2 The Free Education Allowance of Each Education Stages between Regular and Inclusive Students in Private School in Recent Academic Years[89]

Student Type / Degree		2011/2012		2012/2013		2013/2014	
		Regular Student	Inclusive Student	Regular Student	Inclusive Student	Regular Student	Inclusive Student
Preschool		22,800.00 MOP	45,600.00 MOP	24,200.00 MOP	48,400.00 MOP	30,200.00 MOP	60,400.00 MOP
Primary school		24,000.00 MOP	48,000.00 MOP	25,600.00 MOP	51,200.00 MOP	32,300.00 MOP	64,600.00 MOP
Middle school	1st year	22,000.00 MOP	44,000.00 MOP	32,800.00 MOP	65,600.00 MOP	40,300.00 MOP	80,600.00 MOP
	2nd year			23,450.00 MOP	46,900.00 MOP		
	3rd year						
High School		24,900.00 MOP	49,800.00 MOP	26,600.00 MOP	53,200.00 MOP	45,700.00 MOP	91,400.00 MOP

The above data is arranged from the database of the official website of the DSEJ. As we can see from the statistics above, the free education allowance of each inclusive student is doubled compared with the regular student. This is

---

[89] See official statistics of the DSEJ http://portal.dsej.gov.mo/webdsejspace/internet/Inter_main_page.jsp#; accessed on 15th of August, 2014; the materials are rearranged and translated by the author.

the financial support from the government to each student, and we can see not only the support for each student with special education needs (inclusive student) has twice amount than the regular student, but the trend of education funding of the total amount is increasing in a tremendous speed.

5.5.2 The missing regulation of the cost issue

The above forms and statistics tell us that the government pays lots of money to support the development of special education and provides plenty of services to ensure the implementation of the Decree Law No.33/96/M and related regulations going in a right direction. The free education allowance is assigned by the government to cover the educational fee from school; the extra allowance is for the coverage of the fee for schools to hire resources teachers and the related services providers and so forth.

All these actions are done by the DSEJ and schools, when we analyze the Law No.9/2006 and the Decree Law No. 33/96/M, which regulating the implementation of special education, we would find there is only one article mentions the cost issue.[90] Even worse, the article says that the government should create conditions for special education development, and financial support is one of the methods to achieve the responsibility from the government. This is not an operational article and it is like an advocate or a slogan more than a legal provision. Unlike the Taiwan Special Education Law, it states the special education budget, to some extent, should be no less than 4.5% of the yearly educational budget in the central government and no less than 5% in the local government.[91] This is an operational article for implementation. It gives the authorized institute a certain limitation to divide

---

[90] The Law Number 9/2006 (the Macau Fundamental Law of Non-Tertiary Education System), Paragraph 5 of Article 12.

[91] The Taiwan Special Education Law, Article 9; legislated in 1984, amended in 2013.

the proportion of financial budget, and this article would stabilize the development of special education on the financial support.

Occasionally, the cost issue is a sensitive topic and lots of cost will be occurred while implementing special education. If the only legal foundation is an advocate article, it would cause some incompetency in the student's education. A vague law causes a legal gray area shadowing the education of students with special education needs and the family with children needing special education. In addiction, the cost issue of whether a particular special education and related services cost would be determined by the government but not the Decree Law No.33/96/M and related laws due to the missing detailed provision of the cost issue.

There are no operational articles directing on how to solve the problem of who should be responsible for the fees of special education. Is not that necessary for us to think about would it be more appropriative and adequate if the law regulates the cost issue of special education in a more detailed way? However, nowadays in Macau, most of the expense by special education is paid by the government, the education life of students with special education needs is safeguarded by the government relying on the Subparagraph 1 of Paragraph 1 of Article 12 of the Law No.9/2006.

As far as the author is concerned, the blank of cost issue in the Decree Law No. 33/96/M puts the students and parents in a situation without legal protection while facing the cost issue. Since the law gives the government its dominance in funding the special education institutes and students, the law must consider that the government is the most qualified legal personnel on the cost. But on the other side, we can see there is no way for students with special education needs and their families and the special education institutes who have no legal basis to argue for the cost issue once the DSEJ says it is not included in the government's responsibility of financial support in special education. This may be not transparent enough to protect the legal right of students with special education needs, and further more, the positions among government, special education institute, students with special education needs and their families are not equal, because the law gives the dominating position to the government. Once the regulation about cost issue in legal system can be standardized, we may take it as a good step to balance the situation and it may be a better protection for the education right of student in future.

Chapter Six
Conclusion

There are two main laws regulating the implementation of special education in Macau. One is the Law No.9/2006 (the Macau Fundamental Law of Non-Tertiary Education System); the other is the Decree Law No. 33/96/M (the Macau Decree Law of Special Education System).

The defects of the legal system bring some problems to the implementation of special education in Macau. The most obvious defect of special education law is that the Decree Law No. 33/96/M falls far behind from the reality. The Decree Law No. 33/96/M was put into enforcement 18 years ago and became rigid to the development of special education. As we can see the statistic for the official website that a certain amount number of students with special education needs are influenced by the Decree Law No. 33/96/M in the legal system. Since the Government of the People's Republic of China resumed its sovereignty over Macau on December 20th, 1999, the society has changed greatly.

Even the Law No.9/2006 was put into enforcement in 2006, through the thesis; we still can find it is not enough for the protection of the education right of the students with special education needs. Not only the students with special education rights is not well protected by the Decree Law No. 33/96/M but also the rights and obligations of the parents, the teachers and the related services providers are not well regulated by it as well. These individuals have not enough legal bases to rely on. Once there are legal problems related with special education, these individuals will be put into a very passive situation. The procedures of the implementation special education are essential to the students. How to ensure the scientific and the efficiency of the procedures becomes a legal issue for us to think about. The legislation should take some responsibility to regulate the procedures of the implementation of the special education so that every steps of the implementation can be trustworthy and reliable. We believe the coming legislation of special education law in Macau will be careful about the defects that we have discussed in the thesis.

Bibliography

Monographs

1. Rothstein Laura F. & Johnson Scott F. ed., Special education law; 4th Ed, (Thousand Oaks, CA: Sage Publications, 2010);

2. Li Qingliang (李慶良), ed., Administration and regulation of Special Education (特殊教育行政與法規 [電子資源]), (Taipei: airiti Books Pub, 2004);

3. Zhang Xiulan, China's Education Development and Policy, 1978-2008, (China. Leiden: Brill,. 2011);

4. Cohen Matthew D, A Guide to Special Education Advocacy: What Parents, Clinicians, and Advocates Need to Know, (London: Jessica Kingsley Publishers, 2009);

5. Yell Mitchell L, The law and special education, 3rd Ed, (Upper Saddle River: Pearson, 2012);

6. Daugherty Richard F, Special Education: A Summary of Legal Requirements, Terms, and Trends, (Westport, Conn: Bergin & Garvey, 2001);

7. Burton Mary Ann T, Special Education in the 21st Century, (In Education in a Competitive and Globalizing World Series. New York: Nova Science Publishers; 2010);

8. Travers Joseph & Day Thérèse, Special and Inclusive Education: A Research Perspective, (Oxford: Peter Lang, Internationaler Verlag der Wissenschaften; 2012);

9. Lau Sin Peng, translated by Sylvia S. L. Ieong, Victoria L.C. Lei, A history of education in Macao, (Publisher: Macau: University of Macau, Faculty of Education, 2009);

10. Bray Mark, Higher education in Macau: Growth and strategic development, (Comparative Education Research Centre, the University of Hong Kong, 2002);

11. Marilyn Friend, Special education: contemporary perspectives for school professionals, 2nd Ed, (Boston, MA: Pearson / Allyn and Bacon, 2008);

12. Allan G. Osborne Jr. & Charles J. Russo, Discipline in special education, (Thousand Oaks, CA: Corwin Press / SAGE, 2009);

13. Michael Farrell, Foundations of special education [electronic resource]: an introduction, (Chichester, UK ; Malden, MA: Wiley-Blackwell, 2009);

14. Anthony F. Rotatori, Festus E. Obiakor & Jeffrey P. Bakken, History of special education [electronic resource], (Bingley, U.K: Emerald, 2011).

15. Chen Fenglian, The General Situation of Macau Special Education, (The Macau Education and Youth Affairs Bureau, 1999).

Journals

1. Ruan Bangqiu, "Macau Special Education: Review and Hope", Administration, Vol.21 Issue79, 2008, pp81-104;

2. Sun Weixia, "The Inclusive Education: Concepts and Practice", Mei Tan Higher Education, Vol.21 No.3, May 2003, pp23-25;

3. Chen Fenglian, "The rapid development of Macau special education", Modern Special Education, 1999, pp3-6;

4. Chiuho So, "Perspective towards Inclusive Education in Macao", US-China Education Review, Vol.2 No.11 (Serial No.12), November 2005, pp52-64;

5. Diana Cheng Man Lau & Pong Kau Yuen, "The development of special education in Macau", International Journal of Special Education, Vol.25 No.2, 2010, pp119-126;

6. Phillips Ron, "Forgotten and Ignored: Special Education in First Nations Schools in Canada", Canadian Journal of Educational Administration and Policy, Issue106, June 2010, pp1-26;

7. Guo Meiman, "Analysis of Special Education Law", Special Education of Primary School, No.53, June 2012, pp13-23;

8. Shang Xiumei (商秀梅), "The brief of the legal system structure of the special education in Taiwan" (臺灣地區特殊教育法制體系建設簡述), Modern special education (現代特殊教育), October 2006, pp36-37;

9. Hsiu-Chi Guo, "Discussion on the Strategies for the Gifted Education of Taiwan", School Administration Research Association, R.O.C. Bimonthly Newsletter of School Administration Research Association (SARA), September 2009, pp154-175;

10. Hu Yongchong, "The Review of 98-year Edition of Special Education Law", Special Education of Primary School, No.49, June 2010, pp1-9;

11. Gu Dingqian, "The analysis of the articles related with special education in the Compulsory Education Law", Chinese Journal of Special Education (Monthly), No.5 (Serial No.83), 2007, pp9-12;

12. Wang Haiping, "A Study on the Necessity and Feasibility of Special Education Legislation", Chinese Journal of Special Education (Monthly), No.7 (Serial No.85), 2007, pp3-6;

13. Wu Qingrong, "Jurisprudence Analysis on the Definition of Compulsory Education", Journal of Suzhou College of Education, Vol.26 No.4, December 2009, pp66-68;

14. Chen Chen, "A Comparative Study on Regulations of Handicapped Education between New Compulsory Education Law and the Former One", Chinese Journal of Special Education (Monthly), No.5 (Serial No.95), 2008, pp3-6;

15. Hao Xiaocen, "Reviewing and Introspection on Chinese Special Education Legislation Development", Chinese Journal of Special Education (Monthly), No.6 (Serial No.42), 2003, pp72-76;

16. Ryan James E, "Poverty as Disability and the Future of Special Education Law", Georgetown Law Journal, Vol.101 Issue.6, August 2013, pp1455-1503;

17. Gina Choe, "Statewide Special Education Surrogate Parent Programs: Ensuring Quslity Advocacy to all Foster Children with Special Education Needs", Family Court Review, Vol.50, July 2012, p512;

18. Zirkel Perry A, "The Legal Meaning of Specific Learning Disability for IDEA Eligibility: The Latest Case Law", Communique, Vol.41 No.5, January-February 2013, pp10-12;

19. Zirkel Perry A, "State Special Education Laws for Functional Behavioral Assessment and Behavior Intervention Plans", Behavioral Disorders, Vol.36 No.4, August 2011, pp262-278;

20. Skiba Russell, "CCBD'S Position Summary on Federal Policy on Disproportionality in Special Education", Behavioral Disorders, Vol.38 Issue2, February 2013. pp108-120;

21. Zirkel Perry A, "Is It Time for Elevating the Standard for FAPE under IDEA?", Exceptional Children, Vol.79 Issue4, 2013, pp497-508;

22. O'Keefe Colleen F, "Recent Changes to Special Education Law and the Impact on Collective Bargaining", Illinois Public Employee Relations Report, Vol.26 Issue1, 2009, pp1-6;

23. Arkontaky Adrienne J, "An overview of special education law", Hudson Valley Business Journal, Vol.19 Issue12, March 2009, p11;

24. Kim Daniel & Samples Elizabeth, "Comparing Individual Healthcare Plans and Section 504 Plans: School Districts' Obligation to Determine Eligibility for Students with Health Related Conditions", Urban Lawyer, Vol.45 Issue1, 2013, pp263-279

25. Romberg Jon, "The Means Justify the Ends: Structural Due Process in Spcial Education Law", Harvard Journal on Legislation, Vol.48 Issue 2, 2011, pp415-466;

26. Seligmann Terry Jean, "Sliding Doors: The Rowley Decision, Interpretation of Special Education Law, and What Might Have Been", Journal of Law & Education, Vol.41 Issue1, January 2012, pp71-94;

27. Jameson J. Matt & Huefner Dixie S, "Highly Qualified special educators and the provision of a free appropriate public education to students with disabilities", Journal of law & education, Vol.35 Issue1, January 2006, pp29-50.

28. Sullivan Jeremy R & Castro-Villarreal Felicia, "Special education policy, response to intervention, and the socialization of youth. (Education for All Handicapped Children Act of 1975)(Individuals with Disabilities Education Act) (No Child Left Behind Act of 2001)", Theory into Practice, Vol. 52 Issue 3, 2013, p180;

29. Ben-Porath Sigal, "Defending Rights in (Special) Education", Educational Theory, Vol.62 Issue1, February 2012, pp25-39;

30. Sheng-Ru Wu (吳勝儒), Jin-Xing Qiu (邱進興), Guo-Sheng Zhou (周國生) & Xi-Hui Chen (陳錫輝), "The Characteristics of the Act of Special Education Revision in Taiwan", Journal of Disability Research, Vol.8 Issue1, 2010, pp18-24;

31. Pang Wen, "A Review of Researches on Special Education Law and Legislative Suggestions", Journal of Ningbo University (Educational Science Edition), Issue 4, 2011, pp13-16;

32. Yu Dezheng (余德政), & Chen Mincong (陳明聰), "Two Cases of U.S.A. Supreme Court Justice about Related Services as the Examples to Review the 'Related Service' Mentioned in the Special Education Act in Taiwan", Forum of Special Education (特教論壇), Vol.13, 2012, pp80-92;

33. Kim Fong Poon-McBrayer & Ping-man Wong, "Inclusive education services for children and youth with disabilities: Values, roles and challenges of school leaders", Children and Youth Services Review Children and Youth Services Review, Vol.35, 2013, pp1520-1525, journal homepage: www.elsevier.com/locate/childyouth;

34. Wang Sisi & Lei Jianghua "The inclusive education and enlightenment" (澳

門的融合教育及啟示), A Journal of Modern Special Education, May 2009, pp40-41;

35. Jin Xianghua, "The Research of The Transformation of Development of Korean Special Education", Education Comments, No.5, 2010, pp163-165;

36. Hu Xiaoyi, "Indiscriminative Evaluation in Special Education Law in the United States and Its Implications China", Chinese Journal of Special Education (Monthly), No.2 (Serial No.56), 2005, pp13-17;

37. Huang Yongxiu & Zhao Bin, "Policy and Regulation of American Pre-school Special Education and Enlightenment" Chinese Journal of Special Education (Monthly), No.1(Serial No.97), 2008, pp5-7;

38. Marston Douglas, "A comparison of inclusion only, pull-out only, and combined service models for students with mild disabilities", The Journal of Special Education, Vol.30 Issue2, 1996, pp121-132;

39. Lau, Diana Cheng Man & Yuen, Pong Kau, "The Development of Special Education in Macau", International Journal of Special Education, Vol.25 No.2, 2010, pp119-126;

40. Hourigan Ryan M, "Intersections between School Reform, the Arts, and Special Education: The Children Left Behind", Arts Education Policy Review, Vol.115 No.2, 2014, pp35-38;

41. Takala Marjatta & Ahl Astrid, "Special Education in Swedish and Finnish Schools: Seeing the Forest or the Trees?", British Journal of Special Education, Vol.41 No.1, March 2014, pp59-81;

42. Nguyen & Huong Tran, "General Education and Special Education Teachers Collaborate to Support English Language Learners with Learning Disabilities", Teacher Education, Vol.21 No.1, 2012, pp127-152;

43. Johnson, Evelyn & Semmelroth, Carrie Lisa, "Special Education Teacher Evaluation: Why It Matters, What Makes It Challenging, and How to Address These Challenges", Assessment for Effective Intervention, Vol.39 No.2, March 2014, pp71-82;

44. Anastasiou Dimitris & Keller Clayton E, "Cross-National Differences in Special Education Coverage: An Empirical Analysis", Exceptional Children, Vol.80 Issue3, 2014, pp353-367;

45. Wei Xiaoman, "A Review on the Laws and Regulations of Assessment in American Special Education Legislation", Chinese Journal of Special Education (Monthly), No.10 (Serial No.64), 2005, pp73-76;

46. Li Weigang, "Special Education Legislation in U.S.A. and the Implement-ation to Our Country", Chinese Journal of Special Education (Monthly), No.8 (Serial No.98), 2008, pp11-14.

47. Liu Xianwei, "Inclusive Education Calls for the Perfection of Policy and Legislation for Special education In China", Chinese Journal of Special Education (Monthly), No.8 (Serial No.86), 2007, pp3-7.

48. Lin Xiaohong & Wu Roufei, "Comparison of Higher Education Laws for the Handicapped", Journal of Honghe University, Vol.6 No.4, August 2008, pp78-81;

49. John C. Begeny & Brian K. Martens, "Inclusionary education in Italy : a literature review and call for more empirical research", Remedial & Special education, 2007, pp80-94;

50. Wendolyn C & Lessie C, "Social skill self-assessments by adolescents with hearing impairment in residential and public schools", Remedial & Special education, 1999, pp30-41;

51. Kluwin T. N, "Coteaching deaf and hearing students : Research on social integration", American Annals of the Deaf, Vol.144, 1999, pp339-344;

52. Katie Shultz Stout, "Special Education Inclusion", http://weac.org/the Articles/specialedinc/ accessed on 17th of September, 2014.

Documents

RESULTS OF THE CENSUS 2011 (人口普查), Macau: DSEC (04/2012)

Website

1. http://ccadvog.com/cc/?p=670;
2. http://www.dsec.gov.mo/default.aspx?noredirect=true;
3. http://portal.dsej.gov.mo/webdsejspace/internet/Inter_main_page.jsp#;
4. http://www.dsec.gov.mo/default.aspx?noredirect=true;
5. http://www.unicef.org/about/who/index_history.html;
6. http://www.dsej.gov.mo/cappee/cappee08/se/se5.html;
7. http://www.unescobkk.org/education/inclusive-education/what-is-inclusive-education/background/;
8. http://wenku.baidu.com/link?url=RlR3baUGtvuJJJlXPGpn_Tcxng1KVgr9zN7rBUgLwQcQRNsgswlMFzunrv83__rJNVra_Cz4gUKtJ82G9icxK6ipMkTvnm5SshEZqkKvt1C;
9. http://portal.dsej.gov.mo/webdsejspace/internet/Inter_main_page.jsp#;
10. http://ccadvog.com/cc/?p=670.